YOU NEVER GET OUT

MEMORIES OF TWO PSYCHIATRIC HOSPITALS

ROGER GRAINGER

Order this book online at www.trafford.com
or email orders@trafford.com

Most Trafford titles are also available at major online book retailers.

Printed in the United States of America.

ISBN: 978-1-4907-1672-5 (sc)
ISBN: 978-1-4907-1673-2 (e)

Trafford rev. 10/11/2013

 www.trafford.com

North America & international
toll-free: 1 888 232 4444 (USA & Canada)
fax: 812 355 4082

TABLE OF CONTENTS

PREFACE

This book is in two parts, the first of which is almost entirely memory, as it is an attempt to re-live some of the things which happened to me a long time ago. The second part (which was written first) describes things happening at the time of writing, over twenty years ago, in the late 1980s. Both are now memory.

At the same time, both views remain relevant to the state of affairs existing today in the field of mental health. Together they represent an era within this branch of medicine, one which began at the turn of the 18th Century and lasted until the final quarter of the 20th: the age of the great asylums.

At this point, most will react by saying that this is a good thing, as nobody wants places like that any more, do they? We are less eager to say that we don't need them, however, if only to protect people like ourselves from those whose behavior we find unacceptable, even if not actually criminal. The old hospitals served us as containers for individuals we wished to exclude without actually punishing—or not officially. In fact, the threat of committal to the local mental hospital served as a convenient sanction which could be held over the heads of disobedient children and adults held to be 'awkward,' in the sense of non-compliant.

It was a case of 'out of sight, out of mind.' However much we may deplore such an attitude, it was, and is, definitely understandable. Such places were there to be used, and the qualifications for occupancy appeared to be very largely a matter of opinion; diagnostic criteria were—and still are—disturbingly inexact, and doctors frequently disagreed with one another. Most of all those of us who are supposedly sane have never really known what to do with people who seem incapable of seeing sense, and remain firmly in the way of those who can! In this case, as in others, doctors provide medical solutions to what is really a social problem.

The problem remains, of course. It is only this particular solution which has been abandoned. 'Community Care' now offers a more humane way of providing support for those who have difficulty managing to deal with their thoughts and feelings—and consequently their behavior—in ways which other people find acceptable. The difficulty is, of course, is that such provision is made within the community itself and even doctors agree that mental illness is largely a social malady, affected by social relationships even if not always caused by them. While hospital treatment remains available for the seriously ill the present system, in which patients are regarded as 'users of psychiatric services,' appears to many people to bring the problem uncomfortably close to home.

I myself have experience of this system, both as 'user' and therapist, and have written about it elsewhere (*Laying the Ghost*, 2009). This is not the place to assess its advantages or criticize its shortcomings. This book deals with a state of affairs which has gone for ever. I, certainly would certainly not wish to see it re-established. At the same time, anxiety about mental illness has increased. Is this because the idea of it is ungraspable, for no-one is able to remain calmly reasonable in the presence of a phenomenon defined as synonymous with unreason? Or is it because we have dispensed with one way of trying to control our fear of madness—by locking it safely out of sight in premises designed to reassure us of our own security—and yet have failed to find any convincing replacement? At the time of writing, the accommodation most likely to be provided for someone who has had a severe outburst of mental illness is a prison cell.

What follows is not any kind of attempt to arrive at an answer to these questions, but simply an account of my own experience of two different hospitals, both of them County Asylums, which I have brought together for reasons which are almost all personal, including a desire to offer evidence as to what these institutions were like during the final half-century of their existence, a time of radical change in our treatment of, and attitude towards, people suffering from mental illness. Some, reading this, may well be shocked what they find; others may be reassured. I imagine that many people will be surprised by some of the things I have recorded here. I would be surprised if they were not.

INTRODUCTION

Very few people have a good word to say for the old psychiatric hospitals. Even when they were first built a powerful section of the medical profession questioned the wisdom of attempting to alleviate psychiatric distress by keeping so many sufferers all confined in the same building. The general public, however, were relieved to have the mentally ill taken off their hands. This, in fact, has been the way that such hospitals have been regarded: as unloading places, dumping grounds. As such it was obviously important to keep them at arms length, away from 'normal' people. With rejection, fear followed automatically. Mental illness was aversive enough: the place where it was kept had the fascination of the forbidden and untouchable. And so it must be, if one was to remain unsullied.

Now the doors are open. They have been for some time, in fact. Strangely enough, not everyone wanted to leave. Now government policy is forcing them out, as the hospitals themselves begin to close down. No-one sheds a tear for them; their value is simply that represented by the price of the land they occupy. This would be used to provide facilities for ex-patients—but obviously it couldn't happen until the patients had first of all been cleared out.

In the light of the new state of affairs—that of having to cope with large incursions of ex-hospital patients, most of whom were still receiving treatment, some of whom had nowhere to live—people began to look back upon the old system in a more kindly way. Very few shed any tears for the huge psychiatric hospitals, however. It was simply better than nothing. Writing in 1983, Dr S. Winfield said:

Whatever reservations there are about . . . Hospital, at least it exists . . . Its closure is a risky and experimental move, which should have been funds and planned accordingly. Instead, it is run down before alternative services exist (Winfield, 1983).

'At least it exists.' There is more to be said in favor of these hospitals which, for the wrong reasons, have suddenly become so valuable again. In this book I shall suggest a more positive view—one which sees these institutions as places devoted to the task of caring personally for those to whom it is not always easy to feel much love—and most people don't even try.

PART I

PROLOGUE

1 FROM THE INSIDE OUT

The long row of hospital beds faced the walled exercise yard. Between them and the enclosed space, permitting a glimpse of sky and the tops of a few trees, was an iron lattice-work grille. A row of beds, a strip of highly polished parquet flooring, an iron barrier, an empty stone-flagged court, a high brick wall, a ribbon of sky. When I think about Hillside Hospital, I remember rows and strips of things: beds, tables, knives, forks and mugs, patients. It was like a crazy parody of the time I spent as a National Serviceman in the army, with a narrow walled court substituted for the wide open asphalt parade ground and lines of tall, red brick buildings for the rows of low black Nissen huts. There were no nights off in the town here, though, no evenings spent drinking espresso coffee or trying to whip up courage to accost the local girls outside the Ritz cinema, only evenings spent listening to my fellow patients as they recounted their own individual versions of 'the plot'—the universal conspiracy on the part of society in general, and their own families in particular, to deprive them of their liberty by pretending that they were insane and must be kept forever under strict surveillance.

In our case, this surveillance was carried out by Mr Wilcox, a great sergeant major of a charge nurse who completely dominated the ward and terrified most of the inmates. Well, he terrified me, at least. I thought him intolerant and vengeful, motivated by a smoldering determination to exact satisfaction from the unfortunate people under his care, to teach them a lesson for being mentally ill that they would never forget. I couldn't help comparing him with my sergeant at the camp, who had shown such a surprising capacity for understanding and patience when I first began to 'crack up.' It was certainly a smart ward; the tables and chairs in the day room, where we ate our meals and held stilted conversations with the frightened relatives who came to visit us, were all neatly set out, not a table or chair or a knife and fork out of place, the parquet floor burnished to a high gloss by our efforts to polish it in accordance with the specifications laid down by the Charge Nurse.

This involved working away for hours on end with an instrument known as a 'bumper.' It resembled a broom with an extra large handle and a heavy cylindrical block of wood fixed on the end in place of the broom-head, a piece of cloth soaked in liquid floor polish bound round it. You couldn't just use the bumper. You had to learn how to use it, and this wasn't easy because it meant swinging the whole contraption from hand to hand in a wide circle, so that first one arm and then the other was almost dragged from its socket by the weight of the bumper head as it struck the floor. Left, right, left, right—even at this distance it makes my arms ache to think about it. Writing about that time is not an easy thing to do. As I think about it I begin to feel it all again, and my body recalls things I had imagined that it had forgotten. The slide and bang of the bumper, the smell of the polish, the diamonds of sunlight cast on the parquet floor by the iron grille. 'Make it shine like the sun!' I remember the long round of bed making which took place every morning with its endless 'hospital corners:' even now I want to re-make every bed I see which hasn't got 'hospital corners.' I remember the piles of crockery in the ward kitchen and the unique kitchen smell. Remembering, I am aware of the peculiar emotional tone which characterizes everything. This ward expresses a universe of feeling. The memory exudes an atmosphere which is intensely powerful and yet surprisingly difficult to describe: a comforting sort of terror. I was locked in and it didn't seem likely that I would ever get out. Even if I got off the ward, I would never leave the hospital itself. Some of the patients, I knew, worked in the gardens; perhaps I might be allowed to join them, working with a hoe instead of a bumper. This would be an improvement, certainly, and in the circumstances it seemed the best I could hope for. I knew that the hospital itself would never relinquish its hold over me, because everyone said so: 'Once they get you in they keep you in. You never get out.'

Everyone knew that. In a sense, this was not a fantasy, but a true statement of how things were on Bollington Ward. The ward was my world and the situation which existed in it was for me the only possible situation. I was totally enclosed, metaphorically as well as literally. Somebody once said that 'reality is everything that is the case.' Just as I was Dr Houlding's 'case,' so Bollington Ward was mine. For me life had suddenly become extremely simple, and I valued the fact. For the first time for months—perhaps even years—I knew who I was and where I was. Not only this, I knew who my friends were and who my enemies. Everyone on the ward was potentially my friend, even Mr Wilcox—for, after all, he was the ward's originator and sustainer. On the other hand, the people on the outside were obviously enemies, or why would they have shut me up in the first place? Their strategy had misfired, however. I was safe now, delivered from all my responsibilities and anxieties, beyond the reach of the results of my own inadequacy and the intolerable pressure of other people's expectations of me. I was safe.

And yet it was a painful safety: 'You never get out.' However hard I might try to adapt and assimilate, to make the best of a bad job, I shuddered at the prospect of such a final and all-embracing security. The ward was my womb. I was fed, clothed and protected. I had no responsibilities, no anxieties, no challenges. The doctor would make sure that I received the proper treatment, the treatment I needed and deserved. There was nothing I could do, nothing at all. Despite its problems and pressures, the world I lived in until I was eighteen was my world and I had learned to wring some kind of satisfaction from it. I couldn't help regretting its passing away. Deep down I longed to *do* and to *be*, once again. There was nothing here to look forward to but the atoning agony of the room where I received the treatment reserved for people like me: the 'deep insulin shock' which would beat away my schizophrenic delusions and make me a normal person able to live among other normal people again. And perhaps when the course of shocks was over—if it ever *was* over—I would be able to leave hospital. That was what the doctor had told my parents, anyway. The point was, could I trust what he said? Could I believe that he had really said it? I had only their word for it, and my friends on the ward were so positive that of all people, families were the least to be trusted.

Not everyone on Bollington Ward was my friend, of course. Only the ones who were sane, as I was. Some of the other patients were obviously very different from me. They spoke to themselves and beat against the walls, and you couldn't hold a decent conversation with them because you couldn't make sense of what they said. These were the 'mad' ones and it was best to avoid them. (I learned later that in fact they were not as mad as I had thought, despite their dramatic behavior. Be that as it may, they certainly impressed me!) I was terrified of these patients and felt affronted at being shut up in the same place with people who were so obviously ill, so completely unlike myself and the ones like me. In contrast to these folk, my friends and I were obviously normal and sane—which only went to show that something strange was going on here. This hospital was not all that it pretended to be, not all that the people outside said it was. And so I was both sane and mad, a patient who needed treatment and the unhappy victim of a well-laid plot. No wonder I was confused and uneasy. This was the dilemma which confronted me every day I spent is a patient on Bollington Ward.

I was not alone, however. Other people were in the same position as I was. I had friends, and I certainly needed them. We needed one another. We spent the time we could snatch away from our various ward duties, the interminable 'bully sessions so enthusiastically directed by Mr Wilcox, in talking among ourselves, telling others our individual life histories, explaining in painstaking detail how it came to be that people like ourselves should ever have come to end up in a place like his. In this way we grew fond of one another, as people do when they share the same burden and are faced with the same situation. We 'cut our losses' and enjoyed the pleasure of one another's company. Looking back on it now, I can remember that particular feeling very well.

I remember Jim, who spent most of his 'free' time lying on his bed. He would lie there on his back, his hands clasped under his head and stare at the ceiling. There was nothing wrong with him, mind you; he was quite all right, just a bit quiet, that's all. He liked to think of all the people on the ward; he was the one who was most oppressed by Mr Wilcox's bullying. As soon as the charge nurse was out of the room, Jim was back to thinking again. 'I've got to be quiet, I've got to think things out.' I asked him why this was so, but he never really told me. He'd been a sailor for his National Service. This had made a big impression on him (this, at least, I could understand!) and now he wanted to think about it. The only strong emotion he ever showed was directed at Mr Wilcox who, he said 'reminds me of someone.' Most of the time he seemed perfectly content just lying there thinking. Now and again he would make some laconic remark, joining in our conversation from the hospital bedspread. What Jim said was always to the point, always worth hearing, even though, or maybe *because*, there was so little of it. His bed was the most fastidiously made of all, and he shouldn't of course have been lying on it. We never commented on this because we all knew why he did it. It was a classic example of the celebrated technique of dumb insolence—the only kind of military action most of us conscripts had ever been involved in during our time in the Services. You couldn't really beat them, but at least you could make sure you never actually joined them. Not willingly, anyway. We never discovered which particular Chief Petty Officer Mr Wilcox represented, because Jim never spoke about what had happened to him in the Navy, and we knew better than to probe. I certainly didn't try to find out what had made Jim like that. I liked him as he was as did everyone else on Bollington Ward—except Mr Wilcox of

7

course. To be fair, I never saw him strike Jim. He just dragged him to his seat and cursed him. The bawling NCO and the impassive squaddie: both men played their parts strictly according to the script.

Jim never spoke very much at all. He would throw occasional laconic remarks across at us, not actually taking part in the conversation, just commenting on it. Most of the talking came from small sharp-faced man who seemed to be the ward's senior patient. Not the oldest, by any means, for he was only about forty-five, but the most important. I'll call him Frank, though I've forgotten his real name. I remember things about him better than I remember the man himself. He was always more of an idea than a person: as an idea he was clear, precise and terrifying, and remains so to me even now. He had the gift of vivid narrative and a real talent for describing people and places. It was always easy to listen to Frank, and his stories about the things that had happened to him and the people he had known provided the only distraction we ever had on Bollington Ward.

In Frank's stories, fact and fantasy were interwoven in the subtlest way so that you never knew where the one ended and the other began. He had spent over twenty years in various mental hospitals up and down the northern part of England. He liked to tell us about the differences between them from a patient's point of view: the advantages of Rainhill over Parkside, or De La Pole over Prescot, the strange cultural variations of hospital procedure between institutions in different counties, the unique terrors of Rampton itself. Frank was a professional, a specialist in the weirdly fascinating mixture of science and sadism, medical expertise and crass institutional manipulation and repression of the human spirit which constitutes the lore of mental hospitals, the cherished tradition of the psychiatrically stigmatized. Frank had penetrated the barrier which divides the people who have known the joys and terrors of the insane asylum from everyone else in the world, who can only look on in ashamed fascination. It was his duty and privilege—and above all his satisfaction—to initiate the rest of us into his world. It was not enough just to be a mental patient; you had to learn how to think like one, how to see yourself and the rest of the world from that unique point of view. For this you needed a teacher. Frank had undertaken to perform this task and he did it with complete devotion, and also a good deal of skill.

Frank's message, his doctrine of patienthood, was in two parts. The first part concerned the inmates of mental hospitals, most of whom, Frank maintained, were obviously sane. He provided evidence for this by quoting the cases of a whole string of patients whom he had known personally over the years, who by their behavior and the things that they said were completely normal. Some of these people were decidedly above average, in fact.

> There was this bloke at High Royds who taught himself German in six months by one of those correspondence courses. I'm not kidding—there was a German doctor there, he's most likely still there. He thought he *was* a German, used to talk to him in German.

or

> You should have seen old Pete! He was amazing; he'd got the whole ward organized like a bookie's office, putting bets on for all the staff. He even had a bloke with a typewriter to do his secretarial work for him.
>
> Where did he get a secretary from, Frank?
>
> Where d'you think? Another patient used to be an accountant. Came in very useful for keeping the books. No mucking about, though; you couldn't get anything past Pete . . .

Frank's main piece of evidence in support of this part of his argument, however, was his own obvious sanity. We all agreed about his. He didn't need to press the point. In fact I don't remember him ever mentioning it. He was clearly as sane as the rest of the group. And we were as sane as him; the point hardly needed stressing. It was established both by implication and by ordinary observation of the facts. We sat at Frank's feet and he instructed us. He enjoyed teaching us, and we needed no urging to learn the lessons he taught.

The second part of his gospel followed inevitably from the first. If we, and people like us, were sane then either the rest of the world was mad or—even more alarming—its actions towards us were prompted by a straightforward desire to control and manipulate us. Frank wasted little time on the first of these propositions. Why impute madness to men who were so skilled in structuring the kind of world that they themselves wanted to live in? Obviously the doctors and nurses weren't barmy, anyone could see that. They were as sane as we were! The truth of the matter was that the people who were in charge of us and who kept us locked up were no more free agents the we were ourselves. They were the more or less willing instruments of other people's malevolence. Who these other people were was a more or less open question. Having once accepted the initial premise that we were sane people detained against our will by others more powerful and influential than ourselves, we were at liberty to decide who it was that had reduced us to such a position. Frank was quite willing to leave that part to us. He had his own particular theories, but he had no desire to impose them on us. Each of us must decide for himself who was his own personal enemy on the outside and to make his own plans as to how best to deal with the situation.

We were free to discuss the subject among ourselves, of course, and we did so at considerable length, on many occasions. It was a enjoyable way of passing the time on Bollington Ward, and one that we found more emotionally satisfying than making beds and bumping the floor. What Frank said certainly seemed to make a good deal of sense; some blamed the local council for their present position, some the government itself or some particular department of the administration. Most of us, however, blamed our own families, and this certainly affected the way in which we received them when they came to visit us. I can remember those visits very well even now. As far as I was concerned, I would never trust my parents again. It was a painful way of learning independence, and one that was psychologically destructive. As far as my father and mother were concerned, enough strain had already been put on the relationship by my own behavior before I had ever come into hospital in the first place and the shame of having a son 'in a place like that' was guaranteed to make them feel unhappy and anxious and to erect a kind of emotional barrier between us, which took many years to remove—if it ever was finally removed, which I doubt. I remember my mother saying, a long time after I had left the hospital, that she was 'determined to stand by me, whatever I had done,' because I was her son. '*Whatever I had done!*' I understood well enough all these years later what it was that she meant. All the same, it is only now, when I have to write about it, that I appreciate the full implications of her remark.

Perhaps I ought to say more about this in order to clear up any misapprehensions about what was actually going on in these sessions on Bollington Ward. Anyone reading this account who is familiar with psychiatric diagnoses will almost certainly identify our attitude as a sign of mental disease: we were paranoid patients behaving in a way which is characteristic of people suffering from that particular form of illness. I would only say that it seemed to me then, and it still seems to me, that we were behaving entirely reasonably. All the evidence that we had at our disposal pointed in the way that I have indicated. We were simply trying to make some kind of sense out of a state of affairs which was both confusing and terrifying. We could not understand what it was that was happening to us. We had been taken out of our own familiar environment and put in a place which represented all our most primitive fears. We were awake and yet the nightmare persisted. We struggled to preserve ourselves in a situation in which we were deprived of any kind of autonomy, any free action or independent thought. We struggled to be ourselves in a world which contradicted every assumption about ourselves and other people which was precious and fundamental to us. We could not get out and we had no reason to believe we would ever do so, ever again be free to move in the world that had formed us and to which we belonged. Not only this, but we were subjected to all sorts of degrading experiences, including a particularly vicious kind of medical treatment which left us thrashing about in high-sided wooden cots unable to think properly, terrified that we were finally losing our grip on reality and were now permanently insane; we yelled and kicked like demented infants, the victims of some kind of devilish experiment. We had no illusions about what kind of place we had been brought to. This was a lunatic asylum all right. Old Joe talking away to himself all the time in the corner of the ward, the old man in the end bed who just lay there and masturbated—they were obviously mad. But it was not only the patients' behavior that convinced us of our predicament.

The whole situation was confusing. Somehow we had to make sense of it. As it was, it only made one kind of sense, the kind psychiatrists call 'paranoid delusion.' We knew that we were being persecuted because we could find no evidence in our surroundings that could suggest any other kind of explanation. Perhaps the reasons for our present predicament could be discovered outside the hospital itself. But we could not see that far. If we could have remembered the things that had happened during the weeks and months preceding our arrival on Bollington Ward we might have stumbled on some kind of clue which would have helped us to understand why we were being treated as if we were insane. It was always possible, of course, that we had behaved in some kind of way that had misled people into drawing that particular conclusion. It was always possible that they had been acting in good faith and had committed us to Hillside Hospital in the genuine belief that they were doing their best for us and really wanted us to 'get better.' The whole thing—the forced labour, with bumpers and beds, the incarceration with lunatics, the treatment that didn't bear thinking about—could all be a huge mistake! It didn't seem likely, but it was possible. If we could only remember . . .

I for one could remember almost nothing that had occurred anywhere except on this ward and in this hospital. I still had some kind of recollection of my home and family and of things that had happened during all the years that I was a child and then an adolescent. I could even remember bits about being a soldier. But it was always an effort to do this. For one thing the scandalous nature of the events which were actually taking place kept me trapped helplessly in the present. It was as if I was hypnotized by the sheer outrage of it all. I sought escape in fantasy, rather than memory. Remembering was painful as well as difficult. Better not try to remember, better to go on simply imagining.

For another thing, the kind of 'therapy' we received on Bollington Ward made remembering difficult. As the locked doors and iron grille confined us to a particular place, so the Deep Insulin treatment kept us imprisoned in an endless present. On Bollington Ward we passed our days islanded by nightmare, separated from past and future by a seemingly endless succession of insulin comas. 'Deep Insulin' was a kind of chemical shock treatment. You were given enough insulin to send you into a coma and then your blood sugar level was brought rapidly back to normal, bringing you back to consciousness again. Put like that, the process doesn't sound particularly alarming. In fact, it was extremely, even brutally, uncomfortable. Going into the coma was painless. The nightmare came when you were coming out. I found this process of struggling back into life the most terrifying experience I have ever undergone. I screamed and shouted for help, lashing about, kicking the wooden sides of my cot until my legs and feet bled. I was not alone. Around me other patients were doing the same thing. The struggle for consciousness was like trying to run from a blazing car with legs that have had the bones taken out of them, or pulling yourself out of the deep end of a swimming bath when you can't swim and they're holding out a pole covered with grease. Only this was your brain that it was all happening to and you couldn't think what to do because you *couldn't think*.

This was the therapy given to us on Bollington Ward. I believe that Deep Insulin is no longer used as a treatment for schizophrenia in British psychiatric' hospitals.[1] I hope it is not used at all, for anything. I have never spoken to a doctor about it, though, so I'm still not sure. On Bollington Ward we never had an opportunity to speak to a doctor at all. Now and again once a fortnight or so an assistant psychiatrist used to walk through the word, but he didn't stop. As soon as he appeared in the doorway a group of patients rushed up to him, but he continued on his way up the ward towards the door at the other end, trailing patients behind him all the way.

> When will I be able to go home. Doctor?
>
> Have I nearly finished my treatment?
>
> Can I speak to you for a moment, Doctor, I haven't managed to speak to anyone since I came.

The doctor would go out, just as he had come in, without a word.

Memories of Bollington Ward: the iron cots with their wooden sides, colored pink—only to be seen when the door at the end of the yard was open, because when treatment time came we were usually too drowsy to notice; the pattern of the iron grille on summer sky and polished parquet floor; the smell of polish and sodium pentathol and urine and the sight of the doctor's departing figure; the pale faces of my parents at visiting time, my mother's tense with anxiety (I have forgotten what my father looked like); the glimpse of tiled roofs and brick walls if you stood at one end of the ward and looked up and out over the airing court wall. (Although I lived there for six months, I never saw very much of the rest of the hospital. Once there was a dance held in the Main Hall, some distance away from the part of the hospital where Bollington Ward was situated. I asked if I could go, remembering the dances I had been to at our local church hall and how excited I had been by them. Amazingly I was allowed to go, under escort of course, and I made the long journey across yards and along corridors, pausing every few moments for doors to be unlocked and locked again behind us. I don't remember the dance or the place where it was held. I only remember the patient I danced with—not her face or her clothing, the color of her hair or even her age, though I think she was about forty and her hair was going gray, but I'm not sure. I only remember dancing with a woman and holding her close. The picture is blurred by time and the excitement magnified by the hours of fantasy which followed, but the memory of the experience itself is vivid enough and, over the years, my body still remembers.)

I remember Frank and the sessions spent listening and imagining, grouped round one of the little tables out of sight of the Charge Nurse's office, in the part of the ward where meals were eaten. (I can't remember the meals at all, which is surprising considering my rather 'fussy' eating habits—I still shudder at the thought of army meals!) I remember Jim stretched out on his bed completely relaxed, protected from hospital, patients, Charge Nurse and everything else by his own inner strength. How I envied Jim this ability to cope. Perhaps he learned it during his time on board ship in the middle of the ocean. Where are you now, Jim? I wonder if, even now, you could teach me how to do it? Perhaps I might prove a better pupil than I was then, all those years ago.

Legacies of Bollington Ward: an enduring love of group discussions and protest meetings, the opportunity to protest against 'them' whoever 'they' might be, the better side of this being a need to tend other people's wounds and receive comfort in return; a greatly reduced expectation of doctors, perhaps even a tendency to distrust the medical profession altogether, balanced by a deeper understanding of the pressures which they find themselves subjected to; the desire to weep when I see old men raking flower beds; a strong distaste for polishing floors and for the smell of floor polish.

I also learned to be nervous about the smell of sodium pentathol, although this particular anxiety probably stems from the time immediately preceding my admission to hospital when I used to visit the Consultant Psychiatrist's clinic for treatment. I had to inhale this relaxing vapor in through my nostrils and then, when I had slipped quietly away and was no longer aware of where I was or whom I was with, I could let Dr Old into what was actually going on in my mind—with the result that I eventually found myself on Bollington Ward! I always enjoyed these sessions, and even began to look forward to them. All the time I spent under lock and key on the ward, I thought about Dr Old with affection, anticipating the time when I would see him again and he would be able perhaps to explain some of the things that were happening to me. That time came. I asked him if, as I had been in hospital for five months, I might be allowed to go home now. My parents had always assured me when they came to see me that although Hillside hospital was a mental hospital, I was a *voluntary* patient and had come here voluntarily, because I was sensible enough to know what was best for me. I was not at all sure about this, but I thought it was worth asking whether, as it was supposed to be entirely up to me if I stayed or went, whether perhaps I might not be discharged. Dr Old was kind, as he always was. He listened patiently to what I had to say and his reply was gentle. Certainly, I was a voluntary patient, and it was true that I had come into hospital of my own free will. He accepted that, and he wasn't angry at me for pointing it out. Not a bit angry! On the other hand, if I tried to leave voluntarily that would be rather different. He would be obliged to have me certified and he certainly didn't want to have to do that! He'd see how things were going when he saw me again. 'I hope you understand, Roger.' I didn't understand, and I still don't; but I certainly got the message!

There were other, more subtle legacies of my time in Hillside Hospital. Because I tend to be the kind of person who blames himself rather than other people, repressing his own anger by turning it inwards on himself, I didn't actually go on believing for very long that I and my fellow patients were victims of a conspiracy. Psychiatrists talk about what they call your pre-morbid personality which means your 'natural' personality, the way you normally react to things. If you are a patient, it means the way you were before you became ill. My way of reacting to the unpleasant things that happened to me in life is by becoming anxious and depressed. I'm one of those people who are 'their own worse enemy' and I don't readily see myself as anyone else's victim. This doesn't mean that I don't like to play around with the idea from time to time. It provides a welcome distraction from the underlying awareness that, after all, whatever it was was probably my fault. I should have done this, I shouldn't have said that, etc. etc. You can see that this kind of attitude towards other people, everyone in fact who was not in the special group of patients who met around the table in the corner of the ward, provided me with a welcome alternative to my habitual state of mind.

Actually, it did more than that. The implications of belonging to this particular elite were to stay with me and form part of my habitual way of thinking for many years after I left the hospital. I suppose that it couldn't really have happened at a worse time. I was nineteen and what people call a 'late developer.' Emotionally I was very dependent, terrified of having to cut loose from my family and deeply unsure of my ability to survive on my own. In fact I did have an abnormally long list of failures to look back on. At the same time I had been told by teachers at school, and somewhat grudgingly from time to time by my parents, that I had 'considerable' academic ability 'if he could only settle down and find his feet.' How easily the hackneyed phrases roll out, even now. How could I find my feet? I had no idea who I was. Everything I actually *did* was incomplete and unsuccessful.

Only my thoughts were brilliant, unique and properly formed. When I look back now, I see very clearly how typical I was of teenagers caught in the identity crisis of late adolescence, impelled from within and without by the need to create a new adult persona and perpetually frustrated by the shortage of materials to do it with. Their emerging adulthood remains just an aspiration. There is no real flesh to it, no visible newness which can be recognized by others and so established in being, none of the muscle which real independent achievement develops, no backbone of a realistic and stable self-image. No wonder the fantasy of unacknowledged genius seems so widespread and Batman is so popular! If you're imaginative enough and sufficiently incapable as yet to do much more than dream, if you're faced with a world which demands the impossible, and you yourself are so very eager to respond brilliantly to any demands the world might make, you're bound to find adolescence a pretty disturbing time. As I say, I was diagnosed as schizophrenic. I realize that this fact casts a good deal of doubt on the value and accuracy of my narrative, at least from the medical point of view. It means that it's no good my claiming that my disturbed—and disturbing—behavior was the result of the way I was treated, either at home or in hospital. All these things, say the doctors, happened to me because I was mentally ill. And who will quarrel with them?

Who can quarrel with them? It is their diagnosis, their hospital, their signature on the restraining order. Certainly I, and people like me, am in no position to question their actions. If I had not been a patient, not been diagnosed as having a mental illness, it would be different. But who is going to believe a schizophrenic? Just as medication and surgery change the condition of the patient's body or mind, so the professional diagnosis alters his or her social condition. The process of medical intervention is equally efficient, equally *inevitable*, in either case. Subtly or dramatically, doctors transform the human situation. They do so in accordance with their own view of the state of affairs, their own 'diagnosis of the case.' Who are we to complain if their view is a medical one? They are doctors after all. They know about these things, and we don't. We don't know as they know, but we know that they *do* know it!

In an age when all problems of living tend to be regarded as illnesses, psychiatric labels stick faster, and more permanently, than any other kind. The opinion of the Consultant Psychiatrist is the final authoritative pronouncement about the social value of any individual person. The symptoms of mental illness are a useful way of assessing someone's ability to function adequately in the ordinary world of human relationships; the *cause* of inadequate social functioning is the presence in the individual of specific diseases which require their own particular skills to eradicate. There is, after all, a strong connection between the physical state of the human organism and the kind of behavior that the organism exhibits. People who are 'mentally ill' behave strangely; of course, they are at odds with the rest of us and no longer seem to speak the same language as we do; of course, we have a problem and have to find a solution. The question is, what kind of solution? The traditional answer is to say that the problem is theirs alone, and that we have no part in it. This solution has many obvious advantages so far as our own peace of mind is concerned. We do not have to feel guilty for abdicating responsibility, because we are assured that this is the very best thing that we can do for them, and that they themselves will eventually thank us for it when they are in a fit state of mind to do so; we are absolved from the burden of our very natural resentment towards people whose behavior has caused us so much distress, as we discover that it was not their fault that they acted as they did towards us; they couldn't help it, they were ill, they didn't know what they were doing. Again, they'll be sorry when they are feeling better.

Above all, this solution has the tremendous advantage of being self authenticating. If we take the course of action which results in the 'sick' person losing his or her liberty by forcing them to go into a mental hospital, or by putting them in such a position that they have no alternative but to request admission 'of their own free will,' then we will surely discover that we were right after all, for their behavior in hospital will demonstrate only too clearly that they are indeed ill. They will act even more strangely than they did before. Even though they know that it is 'all for their good' they will clamor to be set free; they will refuse to come home again, thus implicitly recognizing their need for psychiatric treatment; even more significantly they will acknowledge their true nature and destiny as sick people by fully accepting the situation in which they find themselves as the one best suited to their new identity as reduced and inadequate personalities and concentrate all their efforts on sustaining the social role of madman to the best of their ability and the limits of their inventiveness.

They won't need to try all that hard, either. The hospital itself provides everything necessary for the role of mental patient to be properly learned. It does this in a setting which seems specifically designed to encourage the particular kinds of behavior associated with people who are considered to be mad. Nothing is normal here:—the patients, the staff or the place itself. Everything is dull and pointless and there is nothing to do which seems to have any real purpose, or that really interests or concerns the patient. Life here is boring and repetitive. The role of the patient inside the hospital itself is always a subservient one. Having lost his place among his fellow men and women by having to come into the hospital in the first place, he finds his self respect wounded still more by the social position assigned to him once he is safely on the ward. He is treated as a person who is inferior and dependent. Everything he does and everywhere he goes his lowly status in the hospital world is brought home to him, not only by the demands of his betters, which he must learn to accede to immediately and without question, but even more forcibly by the tone of voice in which he is addressed.

If you are a patient, mental hospital staff talk to you in two ways, either curtly or patronizingly. Who shall blame them considering the circumstances? Their attitude is founded on the situation which is presented to them and they know as well as you do that you are a mental patient and that it is their job to organize and control your life in hospital. They have to tell you what to do and you have to do it. For this purpose the 'curt' tone is most appropriate, because you might decide to disobey, or perhaps, if you are known to be tractable, the 'firm but kind' approach can be used. On the other hand, because they are nurses and you a patient whom they are trying to help, it is necessary to build some kind of personal relationship with you and this calls for a friendly approach. Because you are a patient the element of condescension is always there and with it the inevitable implications of patronage. Unfortunately this is the surest way of all to kill any real communication between people stone dead from the very start.

Communication in a mental hospital can be very difficult. It is greatly reduced. Because of the restricted scope imposed on normal unforced friendliness by the institutional structure itself, relationships 'within the permitted degrees of kindred and affinity'— that is of staff with staff and patients with patients—can become close and intense. There were some good examples of this kind of friendship among the patients on Bollington Ward. A patient would choose another as his particular friend, taking him under his wing and developing a close intimacy with him. Such friendships were often of the complementary kind in which two interlocking and mutually supportive personalities undertook to throw in their lot together in order to survive the hazards of ward life, salvaging some kind of human dignity by a genuine and unforced relationship. The ward was an impersonal place as the hospital, like all large institutions, set more store by obedience and conformity than it did by human characteristics. The little differences of attitude and ways of doing things, the slight personal eccentricities which make people interesting to each other and serve to give life its flavor were not officially valued here, where eccentricity was always viewed as illness.

This is not to say that it was sternly repressed however. Quite the opposite. I gained the strong impression that some of the patients had decided for themselves quite early in their hospital career that the best way of becoming accepted by the staff was by behaving in ways that other people were likely to consider strange or even bizarre. As mental patients they were expected to be odd. Oddness justified their presence in hospital and consequently that of the nurses and doctors whose job it was to look after them. The observable strangeness of patients' behavior made the whole place more authentic. In this way you earned your place in hospital by reassuring the staff that you needed to be there, that you needed *them*. It was the best way of all to make sure that you were treated with kindness and, just as importantly, that you were left alone.

The rigid division between staff and patients, indeed the whole hierarchical organization of the hospital, tended to produce the same kind of stereotyped eccentricity, according to the principle whereby membership of a group means participating in ways of behavior which are characteristic of that particular group. Social psychologists have made us aware of all the signals, visual and verbal, by which we transmit to other people the vital information that we, too, belong in their group, that we 'talk their language' and share in their particular way of looking at life. These small messages of support, most of which are so natural to us that we hardly notice them at all, do not only signal our membership of a group; they also perform the equally important function of acknowledging, albeit unconsciously, that the group does exist. They underline the independent reality of a particular group of people as far as other people, 'outsiders,' are concerned. These 'outsiders' are not only conscious of their exclusion; they are very much aware of the particular ways in which the group functions—more aware sometimes than the group members themselves. The distinguishing marks of group solidarity show up extremely clearly to anybody looking at the group from the outside. This is one of the reasons why the behavior of groups of patients sometimes seems so bizarre to the staff, who naturally enough, seeing that this is a mental hospital, always explain it as a kind of mental illness. They see identical 'habits' spreading from patient to patient and draw the obvious conclusion—madness is catching!

Whatever my condition was before I arrived, I certainly caught madness at Hillside Hospital. As I said earlier, my experience in the padded cell convinced me that I was indeed insane. I had previously wondered if there might not be some mistake but, once the huge door slammed behind me, I really got the message. I was a genuine mental patient. The quicker I learned to accept the unpleasant fact the better. I have always been eager to belong to any company I find myself in, although I admit that I scarcely ever find belonging easy. Perhaps I try too hard! On Bollington Ward I tried quite pathetically hard. I really did my very best to commend myself to the leading group of patients, the ones that gathered round Frank exchanging stories of their exploits in various mental hospitals. When I had the opportunity, I added my own version of 'the conspiracy of the sane' to theirs. I became quiet and withdrawn like Jim, suspicious and wily like Frank. My eagerness to conform had the added advantage of winning Mr Wilcox's approval, for not only did it confirm my diagnosis ('schizophrenics' are notoriously wily and withdrawn, or at least some of them are some of the time) which as a nurse he was bound to find reassuring, but it also meant that I was considerably easier to 'manage' for I no longer made fusses about being in hospital. Not that I had ever actually dared to make a fuss in Mr Wilcox's presence, of course. But I had been known to ask why I was in hospital and when I could go home again. A pointless exercise, of course, for nobody ever told me. Perhaps they weren't allowed to, or perhaps they genuinely didn't know. After I came out of the cell I didn't ask this kind of question any more. I didn't need to. I knew the answer.

It was never the complete answer because, as I say, I never really felt insane. Or rather I never in any complete sense felt the feelings and thought the thoughts which psychiatrists consider to be symptomatic of insanity. If I sometimes behaved as if I were mentally ill this was more a kind of camouflage than the sign of a deep seated disturbance. Being 'ill'—considering myself to be a mental patient—was only a kind of option which was open to me and which from time to time I found it convenient to use. It was extremely useful as a means of survival on Bollington Ward, for instance. When all is said and done I had all the official qualifications for the role, for I had been in a padded cell and spent six months confined on a locked ward. I had even—almost—been certified! Over the years which followed my release I was to find other uses for this dubious honor!

Release finally came towards the end of my second course of insulin treatment, when I was lucky enough to catch double pneumonia as a result of which the treatment had to be suspended. Miraculously—or so it still seems to me—on recovering from the attack of pneumonia, the insulin shock was not continued, perhaps because I was in too weak a state to sustain it. Anyway I found myself suddenly discharged from hospital. That in itself was quite a shock for, one minute I was on Bollington Ward, gazing through the iron grille at the sky above the yard wall, while the next I was sitting in the back seat of the family car bound for home, free of Hillside Hospital for good.

As it turned out, I wasn't quite free. Not at all free, in fact. You don't shed a new identity, a new life, however easily assumed as that. My role as mental patient, even though temporary, had been too carefully constructed to be quickly discarded. The 'paranoid delusions' certainly vanished rapidly. I no longer comforted myself with ideas about being the victim of a malicious plot on the part of my parents. The habit of thinking of myself as a patient was more difficult to get rid of, however. I was to discover that in fact there was nothing temporary at all about this particular ploy. The decision which I had made, I believe entirely consciously, to be a mental patient and to have at my disposal, as it were, a mental illness was founded in experiences which were horribly real. For a long time it seemed that I would have to live by that decision for the rest of my life, so powerfully was the image of mental illness stamped on my imagination. Never, I thought, will I forget this place. Whatever happens to me in the future, I will always remember it.

In fact I couldn't really remember Bollington Ward for a very long time after I had left it. The six months I had spent in Hillside Hospital opened up behind me like a black hole. I couldn't look back, even if I wanted. I had almost completely lost my nerve. It took many years to find it again, to find *myself* again. The new identity I had assumed hung round my neck like the Ancient Mariner's albatross. When the key had turned in the lock on that winter afternoon, shutting me up, alone and afraid in the dark safety of my quilted 'womb,' I had forfeited more than I knew at the time. The Hospital had custody not only of my body but of my mind as well.

For a long time afterwards I was haunted by a dread of having to go back. Indeed, over a period of almost ten years, I used to wake up screaming in the middle of the night from a nightmare of the most crippling intensity in which 'they' came for me and carried me back screaming to Bollington Ward.

It was not just a figment of my imagination. After I had been home for six months, things came to a crisis again. As far as being able to live together in a peaceful and 'normal' way was concerned, there was no real improvement at all. In fact, things seemed to have got worse. After one particular unpleasant episode, the details of which I have forgotten, my father rang for a taxi and I was put in a taxi, with my elder brother as an escort, and taken back to Hillside. This time I didn't have to stay there very long, but I didn't know that. I remember cowering in the corner of the cab as it sped through the Cheshire countryside, refusing to speak to my brother, who was almost as distressed as I was. It was the middle of winter; I remember the snow hanging wetly from the trees and the sound of the car tyres splashing through the slush. When I look back on that journey along roads that I have carefully tried to avoid ever since, it becomes very clear to me how much I made my family suffer at that time. Michael was four years older than me, and the gap in ages had meant that we had never really been very close to each other. He had his friends, older boys whom I regarded with awed respect and hardly ever spoke to, and I, of course, had mine. Apart from belonging to the same family, it seemed to me that we had little in common. It was left to him, however, to take me back to Hillside, where I was put into a locked room to 'cool off' before being taken back to Bollington Ward. This was my only experience of a padded cell and, as I looked round at the walls, I experienced the deepest despair I have known before or since. Coming into a mental hospital had been bad enough, but *being taken back* was infinitely worse. As I crouched on the floor and stared at the upholstered walls of the room, which had no windows at all except for the tiny inspection pane in the door, I knew that what I had suspected during these long weeks on the ward was finally and irrevocably true. I was a mental patient; I would never get out into the world; I was undeniably and unquestionably mad.

What Michael felt as he drove away in the taxi, I shall never know although something he said to me later gave me a clue. The next time I received a visit from my parents, Michael came with them. When they were making their departure, painfully embarrassed and tight lipped as usual, Michael, who had said hardly anything at all during the interview, suddenly seized my hand and began to shake it. I saw that he was weeping. I asked him why he was crying, because I had never seen him cry before. 'It's because I'm so sorry for you,' he said. I loved him a lot then and I've loved him ever since. He was the only person who ever said they were sorry about what was happening. No doubt they were sorry, of course. Only they never said so. All these years after I am still grateful to my brother for that.

Notes

[1] Editor's note: insulin coma therapy was used alongside electroconvulsive therapy in the 1940s and 1950s as a treatment for schizophrenia among other conditions. See Bourne (1958).

Part II

WESTERN MEADS

2 FROM THE OUTSIDE IN

Twenty years after the incidents recorded in the Prologue, I returned, in the early 1970s, to a hospital like Hillside. This time the circumstances were very different, because I came as a member of staff, the whole-time Hospital Chaplain. What had happened in between would fill a book of its own. Perhaps it is enough to say that, after leaving Hillside, I spent some years as a professional actor, before being ordained and serving as a curate in the English Midlands. I got married and had a family. I applied for the job at Western Meads and got it. I can't remember whether or not I told the church authorities that I had spent time in a psychiatric hospital. Perhaps I didn't; I'm reasonably sure that, if I had done, I would never have been accepted. I had no real intention to deceive, however. I was still very much an Old Vic actor at the time and for me my pre-acting years didn't exist. If they did, they hardly counted now. I couldn't afford to let them.

The memories were there, under the surface, usually emerging in dreams and nightmares. Perhaps this is one reason why I applied for the job at Western Meads—to exorcize the whispers of the past. Apart from this, however, I felt that I probably knew more about such hospitals than the majority of people applying for the job were likely to do. I recognized that this was my job, the one that I had been waiting for all these years. I wasn't sure that I could actually cope with it, but I was certainly determined to have a try, and to try very hard. With all my heart, in fact.

I wasn't at all sure what I would find. How much would things have changed? Would I discover that, horror of horrors, there had really been no change at all? Would my nightmares be confirmed by reality? If so, what would I do? I realize now that this is the kind of thing that people who start work in places like these usually feel. I was lucky because I had actual memories to be laid to rest and I had come to the only place I could possibly do it.

In this chapter I shall try and say something about Western Meads— how it differed from Hillside and how, even after all these years, the old traces of repression lingered on. Perhaps I shall be able to be a bit more objective than I was about Hillside. I don't know. At least I intend to try.

The hospital where I started work as Chaplain 40 years ago was a big one by English standards. It had 35 wards and departments. At its peak, in 1937, there had been 2,700 patients, although the original hospital was built for only fifty. Around the nucleus of that old late Georgian building the tentacles of Victorian growth reached out octopus-like to embrace the spacious park land provided by the hospital's pioneering architects back in 1817. Unlike later mental hospitals, the 'County Lunatic Asylum' was built only a mile or so from the center of the town, a circumstance which reflects a hopeful attitude towards mental illness on the part of the doctors who were responsible for building a 'new hospital for the mentally ill,' one which would help to change traditional attitudes towards lunacy and lead to its acceptance as a form of illness like any other—a condition which could be ameliorated or even completely cured if subjected to the right regimen of understanding charity and strictness of discipline. With only fifty patients, a personal approach could be made to mentally ill people which, it was hoped, would greatly improve their chances of regaining sanity; in fact, the records for the first few years of the hospital's history show a rate of discharge which is almost as high as for the period following the introduction of the new psychotropic drugs in the late 1950s and 1960s.

Much of the treatment in those early years involved talking to disturbed people, 'comforting and exhorting them.' From its foundation the hospital had a large room specially set aside on the middle landing to be used as a chapel. This part of the 'old block' at Western Meads is still called the chapel corridor, even though a newer chapel, the Hospital Church of St Hope, has been standing at the corner of the grounds since 1866. The gospel of the love of God revealed in the deeds and words of the Lord Jesus was an integral part of the 'moral therapy' practiced at Western Meads in those days and the Medical Superintendent and Hospital Chaplain worked together closely as the principal members of what we people now refer to as 'the therapeutic team.' One of the first Chaplains of Western Meads kept a diary which has been preserved in the Hospital Museum; the book reveals great depth of insight into the spiritual implications of mental illness, coupled with a lively appreciation of the recreational value of singing hymns and attending services.

However, it wasn't all sweetness and light even then. There were some intractable cases of mental disturbance for which even the enlightened alliance between scientific medicine and pastoral theology were not able to find a solution. The hospital museum contains examples of the primitive instruments used to control the behavior of the unfortunate 'recalcitrant' patients who could not be persuaded to see the error of their ways by gentler means. Men and women were kept locked up in narrow cells, each with a cubicle alongside to house the servant employed as their custodian, who acted as half nurse, half jailer. When the wooden flooring of the cellar corridor was taken up some years ago, it revealed a long stone pavement sloping inwards from the edges to form a narrow gutter leading to the drain in the center. Prisoner-patients were chained up at the weekends while their warder-attendants enjoyed a few hours well-deserved rest and relaxation. Straw was provided for them to sit or lie down and loaves of bread and dishes of porridge were left within their reach, while the gutter provided the necessary facility for relieving their other natural functions, leaving the attendants to 'muck out' on their return by swilling water down the gutter and scrubbing the length of the corridor with long handled brooms. It would be interesting to know whether the Chaplain ever visited this part of the hospital, or whether he confined his operations to the parlours and individual rooms above, where the more amenable inmates were kept employed about their household tasks. Certainly he could hardly be blamed for preferring the Chapel Corridor to the human stables below and I would be the last to criticize him if he did for there are still parts of Western Meads that I find myself visiting more frequently, and staying longer in, than others.

If you walked round Western Meads on any day of the week you would be surprised and perhaps a bit disappointed by the lack of drama, the sheer ordinariness of the place. Certainly there are long straight corridors marching out like the spokes of a gigantic wheel from the central reservation with its circular observation balcony. The corridors are lined with rows of heavy wooden doors, each with its tiny peep-hole set in it at eye level and its great brass key hole. But most of the doors are open and, if you look inside the room, you'll see a fitted wardrobe, writing desk and dressing table, a couple of bookshelves, probably laden with books, as well as matching curtains and bedspread. People are out and about doing things: playing games in the indoor recreation area (which doubles as the main Assembly Hall), working in one of the Occupational or Industrial Therapy Departments, sitting talking in the tea-bar, visiting friends on other wards, or just going for walks in the grounds, sometimes under supervision, but usually by themselves. In one part of the hospital the residents are hardly ever at home at all, except during the night, as they have jobs in the town or on the maintenance staff of the hospital; even on the Acute Admission Wards a considerable number of the patients at any particular time are likely to be on extended leave, or at least to have gone home for the weekend.

Only the patients in the old people's wards stay at home all day, being too old and too sick to get about, apart from occasional forays into the grounds to feed the cats, or along to the main hall in a wheelchair for physiotherapy. These patients depend entirely on visits from relatives with cars who are willing to take them out of hospital for the occasional weekend, but Samaritans of this kind are few and far between. The majority have no such means of escape from the daily round of rising, having their breakfast, dinner and tea and endlessly, endlessly sitting around in the ward. The ward staff try and make life as interesting and varied as they can by talking to their patients about what's going on in the outside world; a team of 'Diversional Therapists' travels round playing records for a very slow and hesitant kind of dancing, or organizing the more sedentary kinds of ball games, the kind where you stand in the middle of the ring of chairs and throw a padded ball or a soft bean bag backwards and forwards, very carefully. We all do our best to provide some kind of distraction but these are the real inmates of the asylum— the psycho-geriatric cases who make up three quarters of the 1100 patients at Western Meads.

The number of patients is falling all the time, however. When I arrived here there were more than one and a half thousand. By the late 1990s, there are around five hundred. Many have died, usually at a ripe old age, owing to the high quality of care provided here. Government pressure has resulted in a high rate of discharge from among the ranks of the long-stay patients who were capable of being rehabilitated. The Acute Admission Wards, which together make up about one sixth of the total number of wards in the hospital, now function more or less as separate individual hospitals, receiving and discharging patients without transferring them to the old long-stay wards which have become more or less isolated from the acute part of the hospital.

In the old days the Admission Wards were precisely what their name suggests. They received newly admitted patients and assessed them in order to find out whether they would need to stay in hospital for a long time, a matter of months or even years, or whether they could be returned to the outside world to take up their normal lives again comparatively soon. The real work of the hospital was carried on elsewhere, on the male and female psychiatric wards. Because mental illnesses usually take a considerable time to get better and because they are invariably affected by outside circumstances concerning the home and work situation of the people suffering from them—factors lying outside the control of the hospital—most patients who came into hospitals like this one stayed here for a long time. At least patients were safe here and could receive sympathetic treatment at the hands of people who understood their problems. Indeed, a good many of our patients came into hospital many years ago and have stayed here because there was no way of improving their mental condition to a degree which people outside hospital would consider acceptable.

With the passage of time and the development of methods of treatment which are able to modify the symptoms of psychiatric illness and sometimes permanently arrest its course, many of these patients are no longer ill. It has been suggested that a proportion of them were never ill in the first place. Be that as it may, they are ready for discharge and have been for many years. How long they would stay well if they were thrown out of the environment they have known for so long and left to fend for themselves without family or friends in a world characterized by an intractable tendency to reject psychiatric patients is a different matter.

Nowadays everybody associated with mental health is acutely conscious of the dangers of 'institutionalization'—that perfectly normal and entirely natural process of learning to live in a large institution which is mainly responsible for the size of the population of hospitals like the Meads, with their long-stay wards full of people who are no longer acutely ill, but never quite qualify as really well, or even well enough. It is fear of institutionalization, of producing a large number of patients who are adapted for life in hospital but completely unable to cope with the challenge of fending for themselves in the competitive rough and tumble of modern society that has revolutionized psychiatry during the last few years, cutting down the average stay of patients on Acute Admission Wards from six months to a matter of four or five weeks, and introducing what has been called the 'revolving door' system of hospital admissions. The system of extended leave which is widely practiced in hospitals like Western Meads is really a form of rehabilitation undertaken outside the hospital rather than on the ward itself, in which the patient learns gradually to find his or her own feet again in the environment in which he or she actually has to live, with visits from a hospital-based Community Nurse, access to her own hospital doctor and the ward to fall back on if home pressures become really insupportable again. In this way it is hoped that people will not become too dependent on being in hospital, while being able to call for help when they really need it.

A good deal of psychological expertise has gone into perfecting this particular system for helping people who have had 'nervous breakdowns' without making fully-fledged psychiatric patients out of them. Psychology has also played a key role in the battle against institutionalization on the long-stay wards. Here the struggle is not so much to prevent people from becoming too dependent upon the hospital, but to try to undo the effects of years of such dependency once institutionalization has really taken hold. In this part of the hospital, preventive therapy must give place to an intensive program of re-socialization, for the effect of life on a long stay ward in an old fashioned mental hospital has usually been to exaggerate the 'unsocial behavior' which is the main visible sign and principal effect of the very illnesses which such hospitals were intended to cure!

Both schizophrenia and depression are conditions which isolate the person who is suffering from them, even though he or she may be living among a crowd of other people and it is only the primitive need to secure some of the basic necessities of life—food, shelter, clothing—that prevents a person suffering from this kind of illness from losing all contact with the world of other people. In a mental institution of the traditional kind, however, these fundamental requirements of life are supplied with the very minimum effort on the patient's part. He is fed, clothed, housed, cleaned without ever having to communicate with anybody but himself. And such is the nature of the human psychological organism that the impulse to do even that begins to decline through lack of the stimulation provided by social contact and the capacity for it to decay until personal relationships are no longer possible.

According to the age-old way of treating mental illness, people whose behavior is 'anti-social' are 'put away'—removed from the normal socializing influences of ordinary living and confined in an environment in which the basic materials for achieving personal wholeness have been reduced to a minimum. For centuries this symbolic murder has been carried out in the name of therapy. No wonder some modern writers on psychiatry accuse the medical profession of encouraging psychiatric illness in order to keep themselves in business! The results of this kind of policy are to be seen in the long-stay wards of every mental hospital in Britain. Nowadays more and more effort is being made towards getting these patients out of hospital and back into the community. Because most of them have no homes to return to, small groups of four or five patients are encouraged to set up house together, sharing the household tasks and the responsibility for earning the money needed to buy food and pay the rent among themselves. These 'group homes' are provided by local authorities and also by voluntary organizations like Rotary and the National Association for Mental Health. The people who move into them are first of all given an opportunity to get used to living together. At Western Meads we have a house set aside for this particular purpose in the hospital grounds. Inside the hospital itself the work of rehabilitating long-stay patients, re-training them for life outside hospital, continues apace, so that, as new group homes are established, the 'half-way house' will always be kept tenanted by patients on their way out of hospital for good.

Not everybody who has lived at Western Meads for a long time and become 'institutionalized' is able to reach the level of being eventually able to leave hospital. The long-stay wards hold many patients who live lives which are almost totally closed off from their fellows. For these patients the process of re-socialization has to begin right from the beginning. The difficulty with regard to such patients is twofold. They themselves must be given the self confidence needed for survival without the shelter of the hospital and a lifeline provided for them with the place that has been their home for so long—in some cases the only home they can really remember and understand. On the other hand, some kind of support structure must be created for them in the larger community of which they are to be the newest and most vulnerable members. The point cannot be over-stressed. Today, in the face of government pressure to empty the hospital as quickly as possible, it takes a certain amount of courage to try to discover or create life-styles for ex-patients which they themselves consider suitable.

This double problem faces every one of the old mental hospitals. After what seems to have been a rather slow start, this hospital made a good deal of progress. To begin with, the physical environment is very much brighter than I remembered. Some of the wards that were formerly used simply to provide shelter and supervision for long-stay residents were reorganized with a view to positive schemes of rehabilitation, beginning at a basic level. The hospital started to employ occupational therapists to work on the wards themselves, whereas formerly the policy seems to have been to concentrate on those patients who could be induced to 'go to class'—that is, to attend one or other of the workshops in the hospital grounds—while the less co-operative or more withdrawn patients simply stayed on the wards.

More significantly, however, research was carried out within the hospital into psychological approaches to treatment on these wards, where so many men and women sat or stood around for so long, a prey to their own efforts to isolate themselves from all except the most basic contact with other people, as a pathetic protest against the degradation which had overtaken them. Some years ago, in the late 1980s, in two wards in the old part of the hospital, a 'token economy' unit was set up. This is a scheme of treatment, pioneered in the USA, where tokens are awarded to patients for evidence of individual initiative and social awareness—for example, willingness to take part in voluntary group activities. These tokens could then be exchanged for goods at the special unit shop. Starting out as an experimental venture, this unit became an established part of the rehabilitation programme of the hospital. The economic framework, involving the getting and spending of the actual tokens, 'paid off' in another way, and at a more essential level: it was discovered that it was the increased opportunity for social interaction among the patients operating the scheme that proved therapeutic. After a time, people began to do things for their own sake rather than simply for the reward offered. Cases occurred of patients willingly going without tokens in order that more backward group members might be encouraged. In other words, the unit demonstrated that the active therapeutic agent in the transaction was not the prospect of material gain, but of increased personal and social self-awareness. People benefited from getting involved.

I was particularly interested in this. Needless to say, there was nothing like it in my day. Such experiments belong to the situation after the 'psychiatric revolution' of 1959, as do the efforts now being made to enable ex-patients to set up house together on a communal basis, in group homes. I began to understand the magnitude of the revolution that had taken place since I was a patient on Bollington Ward. The most striking change of all was in the area of patient-staff communication. Patients no longer have to depend on "old patients' tales" for their information. The nursing staff spend more time speaking to their charges. The patients see the doctor more frequently. Patients talk to psychiatrists in the grounds rather than having to make a special appointment with a special reason (one approved by Sister, that is).

There is still a lot to be desired, however. Chemotherapy may be effective in modifying symptoms, but it is an impersonal way of dealing with conditions which communicate themselves to the individual concerned as intensely, painfully, personal. In the hospital where I am working, only one admission ward out of five provides any verbal psychotherapy. 'Talking-treatment' is informal and semi-official, from nurses and chaplain, and the only real exploration in any depth is carried out by our psychiatric social workers.

To this extent, then, it must be admitted that, for the man or woman who comes into hospital hoping to be 'understood' by the medical staff, not all that much may have changed. Even though most cases of mental breakdown can now be expected to be of shorter duration than they used to be and the admission units now have little to do with the asylum (which has itself greatly changed), traces of the old system remain. Until recently patients asked me why their clothes had been taken away from them on arrival and I had to explain, yet again, that this happened to everybody and not just to them:—that it was a kind of tribal custom, not a punishment. The ghost of the custodial past still walks here. Its presence is, of course, most strongly felt in the long-stay wards, but patients in the admission wards feel that if they misbehave they may suddenly find themselves 'over the other side' and no questions asked.

Unfortunately, this is not a paranoid reaction on their part. The institutional structure of the hospital has preserved its own traditions—the machinery of repression still exists. And it is used. After all, it is much easier to use force than persuasion, if force is always readily available, and can be plausibly defended and officially sanctioned. This is not a criticism of the hospital staff, who are almost invariably patient, and often sympathetic. It is the corrupting presence of too much easy power, the availability of old sanctions and ways of proceeding, which makes it too easy for problems to be summarily dealt with by main force, instead of being faced and lived through in the community. The person who is the center of the disturbance must somehow live through whatever happens; but it is much more convenient for everybody else if this can be done in the seclusion of a 'secure environment.' In this way, crises of relationship can be avoided. To use four stalwart male nurses to carry an uncooperative patient into a 'side room,' instead of spending time trying to talk things out, is not simply to use a sledge hammer to crack a nut; it is to deprive the situation of any kind of growth potential as far as the patient is concerned—or the staff too, for that matter! Aggression is too often met with aggression, force with superior force.

I notice that, owing to the effectiveness of modern medications, patients do not get as violent as they used to but the old procedures for dealing with violence still exist and can be resorted to for the purpose of canceling out aggression of any kind—even the kind that may be healing in its expression. On one occasion a student male nurse and myself spent half an hour persuading a young woman to go back to her ward and apologize to Sister for losing her temper and flying at her.

Shirley (that is not her real name, of course) had been a patient for several years and had developed the same ambivalent attitude towards the ward sister that an adolescent typically has towards her parents. Sister has had to stand in for Shirley's mother, who had rejected her over ten years earlier. On this occasion, Sister told Shirley to go away, she 'didn't want to see her again,' surely a very maternal reaction to violence! Shirley had gone away, found a milk bottle, broken it and cut her wrists with it. I found her wandering about, had the rather shallow wound dressed and listened to her while she unburdened herself of a lot of stored emotion, before deciding to go back and face Sister.

She returned to the ward, the doctor was summoned and Shirley was immediately moved to Ward 4, the female secure ward, the most dreaded ward in the hospital. I visited her there two days later. She hardly seemed to know who I was. She had learned nothing from the whole episode which could help her as a person, nothing about love, or forgiveness, or responsibility. She had tested a vital relationship and it had failed her. Her worst fears had been confirmed. She had tried to win acceptance for herself on her own terms—for herself as she was—and had come up against a brick wall.

I remembered that wall. The hospital had changed, certainly, but perhaps not all that much. While the old structures remained and the old procedures of social control were available, the specter of the past still haunted the present. I had experienced both kinds of hospital—the old 'pre-revolutionary' one and the one that exists today. They are not the same, by any means. But the old is still recognizable behind the new.

3   INHERITED NIGHTMARES

I said that the old hospital was still recognizable, despite the changes that had taken place in the 1950s and 1960s. For the people who lived in the town itself and the surrounding villages these changes meant little. When the subject of Western Meads came up in conversation in pubs, clubs, shops and at bus stops, people were eager to assure one another that it 'wasn't like that, you know, not now,' before going on to exchange horror stories about what it *was* like. In fact, people still didn't know the hospital as it really was, because it was loth to let itself be known. This wasn't because it was ashamed of itself, but because its main function was to keep its patients away from their fellow men and women. This tended latterly to mean a six-week stay rather than thirty-five years in residence, but the principle was still the same. Protectiveness, secrecy, totalitarian regime founded upon medical authoritarianism and nursing discipline—all these things combined to distance the hospital from the life of the community and to reduce the social impact of the reforms of the 1950s with regard to the treatments and status of patients.

By the time I came to Western Meads its isolation and estrangement from the community was a matter of tradition rather than a reaction to actual circumstances existing in the hospital or reflecting its attitude to or treatment of its patients. That is to say, it was largely a matter of stigma. This is very important. The protective attitude which characterizes everything involved in the relationship between staff and patients comes largely from the knowledge that the main purpose of the hospital is to give asylum to the socially unclean. In other words, as the background to nurses' and doctors' attitudes is the unspoken proposition that 'if we don't look after them nobody else will.' And they're probably right. The exclusiveness involved in having a job most people don't want to do joins forces with the patients' understanding that they are people whom most other people wouldn't want to have anything to do with to form the unique alliance which you find in psychiatric hospitals, the confederation of the stigmatized. This is not a fantasy. People do not care to visit psychiatric hospitals nor the men and women who are patients in them—even when these men and women are close relatives. Nurses and doctors discriminate against professional colleagues who work in psychiatry—if you work *with* them you get *like* them.

On the other hand it could be said that the institution creates the stigma almost as much as the stigma the institution. Psychiatric hospitals are extremely defensive—so much so that they are unwilling to accept outside help when things go seriously wrong. Some years ago, in 1984, Western Meads was involved in a serious outbreak of food poisoning, which caused several deaths, mainly among its elderly patients. The fact received a lot of publicity and the Report of the Independent Inquiry left one in no doubt on the matter. Those who had actually read the report, however, were likely to have received a rather different impression from the one conveyed by the media. The picture of the hospital which emerged there was not simply one of a scrap-heap hospital, in which patients were ignored and neglected, a place of low standards and even lower morale, about which one could honestly say 'abandon hope, all ye who enter here.' On the contrary, no fault was found with the standards of nursing and health care in the hospital.

The nurses in particular were commended for their hard work and for the fact that, in the crisis, men and women whose nursing training was psychiatric rather than general rose magnificently to the kind of challenge no one ever expected them to have to face, the terrifying experience of working on the front line of an epidemic. And not only the nurses: the porters, the supplies department, the domestics, everyone coped magnificently, far better than could be expected. I know because I was there; but nothing, so far as I am aware, was said about this on TV.

Magnificently—but not well enough. This is the picture which came across again and again in the report—that of a hospital stretched beyond capacity, yet refusing to ask for help. The impulse was to avoid fuss, to deal with the situation by ourselves, to draw on those inner resources of toughness and devotion which the hospital knew it possessed to demonstrate at this late stage its attitude of concern for those it served, perhaps, at long last, to disarm people's terrors and win a place in their affections—to be loved instead of hated. None of this could possibly appear in the report. Yet all of it is relevant to the 'breakdown of communication' which it distinguished as such an important factor in the course of the epidemic. What I am suggesting is something along these lines:

(a) the hospital felt itself to he hated, feared and despised. As a result of this, either

(b) it saw an opportunity in the outbreak to redeem itself and win respect if not actual affection by dealing heroically and single-handedly with the crisis; or

(c) it shied away from the likelihood of increased rejection as a result of the outbreak, expecting failure to contain the situation to be interpreted as clinching evidence for the prosecution in the case against it.

Whichever it was, the hospital suffers from a strange kind of institutional neurosis, one which is characteristic of old lunatic asylums, in which guilt and anger, much—but not all—of it introjected, is disguised by a self-protective determination to show how good it is at remaining calm and unruffled in the presence of every kind of disturbance: 'We can deal with anything. We never get upset.' The hospital staff are exceptionally sensitive to the attitudes of everybody who doesn't work here. Like other estranged and stigmatized minorities, they (we) choose to ignore the wider society and look to their (our) own resources, drawing strength from solidarity with others in the same position. This is not any kind of conscious decision. It is more powerful, and more dangerous. It is a state of mind so deeply entrenched within the corporate personality that most people affected by it are unaware of its presence and, consequently, its power to affect a whole range of ideas, opinions, judgments and attitudes and to form the basis of some quite crucial pre-suppositions about the ways in which others are likely to interpret one's own actions and intentions.

Such an argument is un-proveable; however, an overwhelming amount of anecdotal evidence of this kind of thinking within the hospital, and others like it, makes it much more than a mere guess. The evidence as to the high degree of stigma attaching to the hospital is also largely anecdotal, but it would take a very short-sighted and rather foolish man or woman to maintain that this was merely some kind of paranoid delusion.

The neurotic element consists in the transformation of a very real emotion of a negative kind into a positive desire to excel. Even if we abandon such terminology altogether, we are left with a very obvious defensive reaction on the part of the hospital in which threatened people take refuge in withdrawal tactics and the institution 'draws in its horns' and waits for the danger to pass. Of course, we told ourselves that it was the patients we were defending and not ourselves. In fact the defensiveness was mutual and all-pervasive. We had inherited an attitude towards mentally ill people and the hospitals which shelter them in which fascinated repulsion was compounded by professional mystification. This in itself was enough to drive staff and patients together in an alliance against the world outside the gates.

The result of the salmonella tragedy was to make confusion more confused, so that it was no longer possible to distinguish protectors from protected. In the struggle against salmonella and society both groups of people within the hospital had been defeated and their defeat had thrown staff and patients together in a way, and to a degree, that had never been known before. Those feelings about mutual dependency which formed the background to hospital life were reinforced now by an even greater protectiveness, an even stronger sense of domestic solidarity. Staff members were more convinced than ever of an unique responsibility to look after their patients. If they did not do it, nobody else would—for who was going to have anything to do with us now? The attitude was illogical, of course, because it was precisely this kind of thinking that had contributed fatally to the 'breakdown in communications' when the hospital had refused to ask for essential aid and so turned a crisis into a tragedy. The patients, on the other hand, remembered the efforts that the staff had made during that terrible time and were more conscious than ever of the staffs' devotion to their welfare. Protection and dependency are mutually reinforcing aspects of the same social process or, as a patient said at the time, 'we're all in this together, aren't we?' In fact, since the outbreak the institution came to depend more than ever on its own interior lines, as ensuing re-organization led to a tautness of organization regulating all activities within the hospital—and resulting in an even greater degree of dependency.

The social consciousness which produced this reaction in the first place remains totally unmoved by subsequent events. The attempt to defeat stigma only had the effect of increasing it. The hospital staff worked harder than they had ever done in their lives, and society waited to pounce. What is more important, of course, is that the consciousness of mental hospitals as terrifying, loathsome, malevolent places, has rebounded on the actual conditions of patients themselves, who may begin to appear to the staff as people who share their own social curse and so must be protected from those 'outside'—'we're all in this together.' It is a distorted view of reality, no doubt, but one which can have tragic consequences if it results in a self-imposed isolation from help which may be urgently needed. On the other hand, can we really say that the isolation was self-imposed? In the meantime, there is work to be done. Obviously we can't simply pretend that nothing happened, that this disaster never occurred.

Much depends on the arrangements made within the hospital for the rehabilitation of patients. Even more depends on the patients themselves, their eagerness, or at least willingness, to leave hospital and the courage which they can bring to the task of facing the challenges involved in starting a new life, breaking old habits of dependence on the institution, acquiring new competence. But most of all depends on the attitude of people 'on the outside.' The truth is that it isn't only patients who have to be re-educated in order to cope with the new situation. We ourselves, the so-called 'normal' folk, have to learn to adjust as well. We may think that we have an enlightened attitude to people who have been patients in a psychiatric hospital. If we have, we must be willing to demonstrate it. Because there is still a great deal of stigma attached to these hospitals, I'm very much afraid that, if these men and women come face to face with the general attitude of our society towards mental illness and towards people who have been patients in mental hospitals, they may be so shattered by what they find that they will very soon ask to be re-admitted.

The people who live round about Western Meads are very kind to the patients here. If they find an old gent wandering down the main road wearing only his pyjamas and regulation yellow hospital dressing gown, they will take him gently by the hand and lead him back through the gates to Northfield Ward: 'I found him wandering in the street. I think he belongs to you.' But the bus conductor still calls our stop 'Asylum Corner' and it is quite clear from the things you hear people saying in shops and pubs—and churches too—that however much the hospital may have changed, people's attitudes to it have hardly altered at all. Folk still think and talk about Western Meads in the 1980s in the way we used to talk about Hillside

Hospital forty years earlier, back in the 1940s. The gates are open now, people get better much more quickly, the wards and corridors are brighter and more comfortable, there is much less overcrowding, but the stigma remains.

Western Meads, and all the hundreds of hospitals like it, still has the effect of making people into patients. Nowadays this is not because it reduces people to a state of dependency and convinces them that they have sick and therefore socially sub-standard personalities; it is because the people outside hospital demand that it should be so and refuse to have it any other way. It is as if society is determined to retain the concept of the mental patient, as a kind of base-line human condition, a social nadir, the one human status that can't be undercut or downstaged. The thought seems to be that no one can get lower than a *mental* patient, for even criminals are often *clever* people, pitting their wit against society and sometimes succeeding. Mental patients, however, are misfits, outcasts and failures, too inadequate even to qualify for the struggle to survive in a world where it is brain power that counts!

People have a deeply rooted terror of mental illness, comparable to the panic that stops some folk from learning to swim because of an intractable inhibition against relinquishing the vertical position. The position that may never be given up in this case is that of the rational individual, in control of all his faculties. It is a precarious position, and one which we may never be entirely certain that we can keep our hold on, but heaven forbid that we should ever completely loose our grip. We are overcome with horror of the abyss that opens before us. Our fear of madness is fear of the unknown experienced as the *unknowable*. It can only be really compared with our attitude towards our own death. But the image of madness is ever worse than that of death, which can be seen as an end which gives shape to our life, creating meaning from the flux of events, whereas madness is by definition a denial of sense, and renders all previous life, all valuable personal events, futile. Thus madness may be regarded as the invalid event *par excellence*, not just an unreasonable happening but something which puts the meaning of reason itself in question. Madness is total personal disaster.

Its symbol is the madhouse, which is more of a metaphor than a actual location. The madhouse is a more fitting symbol of our deepest and least eradicable loathings than the graveyard, the torture chamber or the prison. It contains elements of all these separate hells of the imagination, combined with its own distinctive anti-rational horror. To imply that Western Meads is like this—to accuse it of being repositories of all that may not be contemplated and should not be mentioned—is to face outrage. But we are dealing with fantasy, not fact, here. These places are both more and less than themselves. Even more than prisons, asylums stand outside the world. As living communities of people involved in the ordinary human business of helping and being helped, caring and being cared for, contributing to individual happiness and the common good, they do not, so far as the popular imagination is concerned, exist at all. As the embodiment in glass, stone, brick and iron of a monumental gesture of rejection their presence is unavoidable, however. So passionate a gesture cannot be passed over or even played down. However many doors are unlocked, however many wards opened, Western Meads remains closed to the real world.

I am talking here of a mythical rather than a literal reality, an intuitive perception which lives alongside our capacity for rational assessment and has a powerful effect on the experience of reality, changing our perception of the truth into something quite different. This myth of madness abides. It is this that sends a shiver down people's backs when the conductor calls out 'Asylum Corner,' that dissuades relatives from visiting patients and employers from giving ex-patients jobs and bestows a strange unwelcome glamor on those of us who work here so far as people 'outside' are concerned. The myth persists everywhere in the world of mental illness. It is to be sensed in 'therapeutic communities' and in the brand new psychiatric wings of District General Hospitals. In great suburban asylums like Western Meads it lingers as an ineradicable atmosphere, a wind from the past blowing round gray stone buttresses and whispering along half deserted corridors and in day rooms newly decorated with bright wallpaper and cheerful prints. No amount of 'upgrading,' either physical or spiritual, seems able to disperse it.

This myth of the madhouse is the background against which we work. The patients themselves all believe it. Their own ward is not like that of course, they would not for a moment suggest that it was; but somewhere else in the hospital, on other nameless forgotten 'back wards,' there are people who are really ill, really crazily insane and *disturbed*. They have never seen these places, but they know they must be there because they have heard people speak about them. It is better not to think about the things that go on there, but just to be thankful that you are not in that part of the hospital.

We have been considering the hospital as the general public regard it—the old 'myth of the asylum' which still retains its power. Sometimes it seems as if the staff believe it too. On the old locked ward the State Enrolled Nurse gladly demonstrates the padded cells along the corridor and explains that the rooms are not kept locked nowadays—'but you should have seen it when I first started here, twenty-five years ago.' She sounds almost apologetic about the improvement. Patients who disobey nurses or doctors on the Admission Words are still threatened with relegation to 'elevens' or 'fourteens,' the numbers by which the old 'recalcitrant patients wards' used to be called before they received their new names. If the unthinkable happens and the threat is actually carried out, however, the terrified patient finds himself in a part of the hospital which if anything is more comfortable and attractive than the ward he has left and where the comparative lack of freedom of movement is compensated for by considerably greater attention from the nurses who, free from the intensive pressure of work on an admission ward, have more time to sit and talk and perhaps build up a real relationship with them. Patients who have spent time on these wards often say that they prefer them, that they feel 'safer' on them. Perhaps the hospital begins to lose its terrors once you reach the center and there is nowhere worse waiting for you if you misbehave. Certainly I have known people break the ward furniture on an open ward in order to be sent back to the security and friendship of one of the dreaded 'secure wards.'

Thus the institution uses its own mythology to further purposes which are considered to be strictly scientific. The secure wards and all that they imply are simply another form of 'shock treatment,' a way of drastically affecting a person's awareness in order to disturb the chemical balance of his or her brain and change his or her emotional state. The principal of the 'short sharp shock,' either surgical, electrical, chemical or, in this case, environmental, has always been the main stock-in-trade of institutional psychiatry. The trouble is that it regards the people with whom it deals as objects rather than persons, mechanisms which have developed faults for which they must 'patiently' receive treatment. Just as a person who has come into a psychiatric hospital is by definition a mentally ill person, so a sledge hammer wielded by a doctor is automatically a scientific technique!

Obviously there is a mythology here at one remove from the original 'myth of the madhouse' and yet closely allied to it as part of the underlying division within human affairs between knowledge and ignorance, acceptability and rejection, goodness and badness. That people are all different from one another is of course a fact but the idea that they can be divided up according to any system of human classification which has an essential significance and refers directly to a kind of underlying truth about human life seems to me to be a social myth. There are no final divisions except those agreed upon as a social convention. There is no *non-cultural* reason why color of skin or religious belief or an inherited fortune or a high IQ should or should not be acceptable as criteria of social merit. Social differences constitute a convenient way of organizing people into groups, convenient that is from the point of view of the group which does the organizing, and which maintains its organizing function in the social system by preserving its autonomy and guarding its frontiers against invasion from other groups of people lower down the hierarchy of groups. The anthropologist Claude Levi-Strauss makes a distinction between what he calls *anthropophagic societies,* which try to contain as many different kinds of people within the community as possible, and *anthropoemic* societies, which relegate non-conformists to inferior status in a lower social group. The idea that a group of people may possess a body of scientific medical knowledge which is more important than any other kind of knowledge and which automatically gives them the social right to make an effective division within society between people like themselves and everybody else is an anthropoemic social doctrine, not a self evident fact of life, although from time immemorial this kind of thinking appears to have dominated Western European social philosophy. When it was not the medical profession it was the Catholic Church, not to mention the Feudal and the Capitalist Systems!

From a Christian point of view, however, the medical mythology is a particularly disturbing one as it implies an approach to human situations which often seems to ignore their fundamental difference from scientific propositions. A human problem is not open to solution is if it were a quadratic equation. Doctors know this, of course, but in a society where the authority of their philosophy is taken for granted and questioned only as an act of bravado, it may be that they need the occasional reminder. It is surprising how our assumptions about the nature of truth resist the attacks made on them by the actual experiences of life itself.

4 CHAPLAIN

My job as Hospital Chaplain was to 'minister to the spiritual needs of patients and staff.' This obviously meant that I should hold services and visit patients on their wards. It also seemed to me to imply a ministry of counseling and spiritual direction. I had no idea how I would get on because I had no experience of work in an institution to fall back on, apart from one or two short courses provided by the Hospital Chaplaincies Council. This was an area in which Hillside provided no assistance; all the time that I was a patient there, I saw no sign of the chaplain, if indeed there was one. While I worked at Western Meads I tried to be as active as I could in his direction, always looking out for opportunities to introduce informal services at weekly or fortnightly intervals in parts of the hospital that were previously uncolonized, ending up with a service on every day of the week in one part of the hospital or another. Perhaps I was trying to atone for the reprehensible lack of zeal shown by my imaginary Hillside Chaplain.

The ability to be satisfied with this kind of competitive chaplaincy was short-lived. It was after all really a distraction from a more fundamental concern—the need to belong in the hospital at a deeper level than that of a provider of services for what was, after all, a very small minority of religiously inclined people.

I wanted to do more at Western Meads than carry out a peripheral function, one that the hospital itself had forgotten how to take seriously. It was a long time since churchgoing had played an important part of life at Western Meads. The splendid scarlet hoods of the Nurses' Choir reposed fustily in the Vestry cupboard. There had never been a whole-time chaplain appointed specially for Western Meads. The situation seemed to me to be full of possibility. I must come to a decision about what my relationship with the hospital ought to be. What was the Chaplain's specific, inalienable, role—the role that, in his eyes at least, justified his being a part of the whole-time permanent staff, employed on exactly the same terms as everybody else? If I wanted to be taken seriously, rather than as an optional extra, I must come to terms with the question and try to find an answer.

It wasn't long before I began to get the beginnings of an answer. It was not a theological one, not, at least, to start with. It was more in the nature of a pre-theological concern with spiritual freedom. You could say that the main job of a hospital chaplain is to remind the people who run the medical institution where he works (and who subscribe to the view of life associated with that institution) that the Christian Church represents a view of human beings which differs significantly from any strictly scientific attitude towards them. The significance referred to is that of the soul: the indistinguishable 'organ' of relationship, at once unique and holistic, by which we perceive ourselves, one another and life itself in a way which eludes description by anybody who is not a poet. The soul is the non scientific entity *par excellence* because it is the organ of human impossibility by means of which we become aware of the possibility of God.

At the same time this should not set the chaplain against the medical institution, for no-one should be more intensely aware than he of the devotion and skill brought by doctors to the service of their fellow human beings, nor have a greater appreciation of the value of scientific ways of using *things* to help *people*. His understanding of the doctrines of Creation and Incarnation teach him how important the physical world is to God, and by the physical world he means not only living human flesh but the machines and equipment and technical expertise used by and for human flesh. Equally important it means the ideas which give shape to human life by producing its physical and philosophical framework, the organizations and institutions essential to human existence—ideas which, too, originated in human flesh.

The chaplain's attitude may perhaps be one of critical appreciation. The fact that he is not a scientist, and yet is welcomed into a scientific establishment, is no sentimental gesture of homage to a past in which religious ideas were taken seriously. Nor is he here simply to minister to people who persist in entertaining an outdated and discredited view of the universe. At the very least his presence presents religious awareness as a complementary and equally valid form of human truth to the one provided by the scientific analysis of experience. Doctors as a profession are not concerned with religious doctrines. However, they must take account of states of mind and attitudes towards life which assume expression in the form of doctrinal beliefs. Psychiatrists in particular are aware of the importance of the symbolic factor in emotional experience. Mental illnesses such as schizophrenia and manic-depression as well as hysterical conditions employ a conscious symbolism to express an experience which originates in an emotional reaction. Sometimes this symbolism takes an explicitly religious form, so that ideas about relationships are communicated in religious language; but the religious element is the form rather than the content of a particular psychiatric condition.

So long as the Chaplain understands this he may prove to be a useful ally of the psychiatrist. He speaks the same language as the patient. He is able to reinterpret the symbolism as a message of love and acceptance rather than rejection and alienation. Often in the case of patients diagnosed as schizophrenic, an experience of personal worthlessness, a sense of the self which has become frail and insubstantial, causes a person to seek refuge in an abstract *idea* of super-human powers which give him or her the ability to rise above all human limitations and assume a god-like omnipotence. Because the consciousness of the self is so insubstantial and inadequate, the solipsistic divinity which our ideas are always able to assume reigns supremely unchecked by 'common sense.' Just as a man or woman suffering from a hysterical condition may assume an alternative identity and 'become' a hero, a saint or a martyr in order to transcend feelings of personal inadequacy, so schizoid people lay hold on the divinity of thought itself. Tragically for them, however, it turns out to be an illusory God, exercised over an insubstantial universe; not only this—because for human beings form and substance, ideas and things, always exist together and are two complementary halves of the same indivisible human reality—the form of his 'divinity' begins to crumble and his strictly theoretical 'power' disintegrates as he loses touch with the content of human life, which is to be a person in a personal world—a limited person in a world limited by personal considerations. The Chaplain's message to such a one is that he is not God, but that he is nevertheless loved by God. The message must always be *about* God, because for this person at least (and for others, too!) the matter in hand concerns divinity: an inauthentic divinity, abrogated by a section of the self which believes itself to be in some way detachable from the rest of itself, and an authentic one who is not, and never can be, the self. He is the divine source of wholeness *precisely because* he is not the self, but the destination outside the self towards which the self directs itself—the focusing point which draws all parts of the self and all separate selves together, as men and women are drawn to concentrate on God as the source and goal of personhood.

The clinically depressed person on the other hand needs no assurance that he is not, and must not try to be, God—nor Satan either for that matter. The depressed man or woman is the person without any kind of power, authentic or inauthentic, ideal or actual. He or she is bogged down by the physical, oppressed by the sheer weight of things, things to be done, things to be suffered, things which simply exist and are there. The center and object of the oppression is the body. When you are depressed to this extent your body is a thing or, perhaps it would be more accurate to say, your body is *the* thing. There is nothing else but the body's objectivity, no free subject, no adventurous and capable possibility of the mind working in and through the body, simply the crippling limitations imposed by a non-functional organism, a lump that should be a person. The human tragedy here is that the lump knows that it should be a person and consequently feels guilty because it cannot be what it knows it ought to be.

> God is there, and I know he loves everybody including me. But I can't *feel* it any more. I can't do anything about it. And pretty soon he'll give me up as a bad job. Which, when all is said and done, is only what I deserve.

It is simple to think of both these states as somehow involving a breakdown of the relationship which exists between mind and body, but this kind of explanation is too mechanical to fit the case. Mind and body are not to be considered as separate entities which have some kind of relationship with each other. A better way of looking at it would be in terms of the ideal and the actual. Human consciousness is a fusion of the actual and the ideal, the established and the potential, what is and what might be. It is possible for us to choose which way we will look at the world, either analytically, ascertaining how things are or synthetically by gauging their ability to change into something else. Our usual way of perceiving the world is by alternating between these two approaches, although scientists often concentrate on the first, leaving the second to artists and philosophers. The point that I am making here is that people who are mentally ill seem to have lost their original flexibility of perception and to have somehow become fixed in an analytic preoccupation with a reality which is changeless and factual, so that failure can never become success and impossibility is always final and total, or a synthetic view in which present limitations simply do not matter, because they do not really exist. You can think your way through anything!

They have become fixed in a particular way of perceiving the world. They are no longer open to persuasion, by argument. The psychology of human perception does not involve the intellect alone, for we 'see' the world before we draw any conclusions about it, and the conclusions we draw depend upon the way we see. *What* we see depends on *the way* we see it. No amount of earnest exhortation or reasoned exegesis of scriptural truth can alter the state of mind of someone whose way of perceiving reality has been deprived of its natural flexibility by mental illness. Clergymen have been known to spend hours not getting through to patients. I know this because I have experienced it myself from both sides of the fence. In a lot of cases the exercise is not completely futile, because in some fundamental way the effort at communication may be appreciated, the will taken for the deed. On the whole, however, it is perhaps better to remain silent, because however healing the message may be for those who are ready and open to receive it—who 'have ears to hear'—it will not be perceived by a person who is mentally ill in the way in which you intend it. Because he or she is not living 'in your world,' every message requires translation and those assumptions about human relationships which are symptomatic of mental illness determine that the process of translation will somehow cause it to be misinterpreted.

All this applies to people who are seriously disturbed and not to those who are beginning to get better. In *Watching for Wings* (Grainger, 1979), I described the experiences, as they told them to me, of people who had emerged from a period of mental illness, and in doing so had become aware of the love of God in a way and to an extent which surpassed anything they had ever known before. This needs to be repeated here. To a person who has recently suffered the spiritual desolation of mental illness, God can make himself known as redeemer and deliverer with an unforgettable force and clarity. Certainly I have personal reasons for asserting the truth of this statement. But I have received identical testimonies from many other people. It is here, at this critical stage in a patient's progress, that the Chaplain may make his most strikingly significant contribution to the wholeness of the people he is called to minister to, as he comments upon what it is that God is doing for the individual man or woman who has come to see him. At this stage the Chaplain's interpretations will be listened to and appreciated, because they correspond to the patient's own understanding of what is actually happening. There is no more wonderful job that he is called to do than this—simply to endorse the work of God and to support a patient's own discovery of the meaning of his illness. As Kierkegaard says, 'Life can only be understood backwards; but it must be lived forwards.' Here at Western Meads I have shared in the joy of men and women for whom both past and future are illuminated by God's disclosure of himself in the eternal present.

This, then, is the 'front-line' ministry of the Chaplain of a psychiatric hospital. He is involved in other kinds of front-line action, too, as he works in close co-operation with others in the hospital in the emotionally charged atmosphere of the struggle against the depersonalizing effects of mental illness. As I said earlier, the ministry of a Chaplain takes place against a background of certain assumptions about madness which still possess a crippling authority over people within the institution whether they are patients or members of the hospital staff. To a greater or less extent, two 'mythologies of madness' affect everybody who lives or works in a mental hospital. These are the *myth of mindlessness* and the *myth of soullessness*. The first of them is associated with too little knowledge and the second with too much—or rather, too much of the wrong kind. The first corresponds to the cloud of unreasoning dread arising from the superstitious terror of insanity which hangs over every mental institution, however enlightened may be the attitude of the psychiatrists, psychologists and nurses who work there. It is the expectation of fear and alienation, the forbidden territory 'outside the camp,' the place of human chaos which maintains its fatal hold over the popular imagination and continues to live on as part of our cultural heritage. We have already remarked on its effects, in Chapter 3.

The second concerns the chaplain even more directly than the first. The second is an automatic and equally unreasoning assumption about the power of medical science to contrive a 'cure' for every human ill, to analyse and consequently control every aspect of human experience, to regard every kind of suffering as a breakdown of the mechanism which can be isolated and eliminated by the exercise of technical skill. The implication of determinism to regard all illness as a failure in the system always results in the rejection of some systems as having irretrievably broken down, so that they are fit only for the scrap-heap. It is the result of too much knowledge of the things that are scientifically or technically possible and too little understanding of the love of God 'with whom all things are possible,' and for whom illness and breakdown are never a sign of rejection but a precise message about the relationships of persons, the divine mystery of loving whose human value increases in direct proportion to its actual cost in terms of the apparent uselessness of our attempts to foster it. The chaplain is engaged in a struggle against ideas of this kind, ideas which have a demonic power over men's lives. He does not have to fight alone, but the terms of his engagement, the ground on which he stands, are unique to chaplaincy.

This is not how most people regard chaplains, of course. The main thrust of chaplaincy training is directed towards the identification and consequent development of particular areas of activity within the work of the hospital in which a clergyman may contribute kinds of expertise that are normally associated with his social role. Certainly this seems an acceptable aim. For large numbers of people, clergy still play an instrumental role at crucial times in an individual's life. A person is not considered to be a proper member of society unless and until he or she has been baptized or married by a clergyman, and the need for clerical intervention is considered to be even more urgent in the case of death. When, in the circumstances surrounding admission to hospital, these life crises appear even more crucial than they usually do, the practical value of the hospital chaplain's presence is clear to most people.

People are not always being born or dying (and rarely get married) in hospital, however. In fact, the chaplain is a necessary member of the hospital staff specifically because he is not that kind of professional. His profession is to carry out, always and everywhere, the priestly and prophetic vocation of the ordained ministry. Thus his presence within the hospital signifies the limited and conditional nature of human ability, the ultimate skill-lessness of human skill. To the extent that professional codes are structures contrived by men and women (but chiefly by men!) to increase the success of their efforts by strictly defining the limits of their responsibility, the chaplain's profession is to be anti-professional. It is this aspect of his role that has been illuminated by the work of Heije Faber, who writes in *Pastoral care in the modern hospital* (Faber, 1971) of the chaplain as a clown, someone whose way of being in the world calls into question the assumptions other people make about the structure of social reality. The clown's antics draw attention to the essentially contingent nature of the toughest systems of social relationship, the most authoritative schemata of thought and action. He introduces the possibility of a revision of ideas and kinds of behavior which have become so habitual as to seem part of the very stuff of reality itself—unchangeable, inevitable, foreordained. I don't know how many times I acted like a clown at Western Meads—but I often felt like one!

The need for clowns is particularly evident in places like hospitals and prisons, which live according to their own private social philosophy and demand the very strictest conformity to that philosophy—who 'worship' that philosophy. Where that philosophy strikes at the root of the Christian gospel, a Christian clown may be more effective than a theologian. Christian writers on the subject of health, notably Robert Lambourne and Michael Wilson, have pointed out that a philosophy of health which attributes an ultimate and exclusive value to the total eradication of human failure and refuses to acknowledge any positive significance such failures might have within the lives of men and women has become associated with the very structures which we use to mediate healing. Such structures deny the humanity of all concerned, 'healers' and 'sufferers' alike. They also take themselves extremely seriously!

The clown is tolerated because he is absurd; in the light of the dominant philosophy of humanistic materialism the clergyman is likewise absurd. His presence in the hospital, the very temple of such beliefs, is more absurd than ever. It is this absurdity which is to be treasured, however. By it, the chaplain is able to 'slip under the hospital's guard' and witness to the contingency of all human arrangements and the unique challenge implicit in every situation which involves people. By it, he is enabled to preach the gospel.

Now that I have written all this I see that what I've been saying is really very obvious. A Chaplain needs to be him- or her-self and to avoid conforming to secular views and expectations which run counter to the Gospel which he/she has undertaken to preach. It did not seem so obvious to begin with; the hospital was very big and the medical world-view very dominant. The answer, however, seems to be that one should take the Gospel seriously and oneself rather less so. More of a clown, in fact!

This is not to suggest that I spent all my time at Western Meads 'clowning about.' There were still those times when my job was to sit and listen, saying as little as possible, times when I was able to utter words of consolation and the assurance of forgiveness, times of Eucharistic concentration and celebration, times of weeping. There were also times for communicating the good news of Christ and of the immeasurable love he brings us. Hospital Chaplains have the privilege of representing the church in a place and at a time when its message is most likely to gain attention. This message may not always be communicated in words, either spoken or written. In psychiatric hospitals actions certainly do 'speak louder than words'—which is why the number of communion services continued to increase while I remained at Western Meads. At these services speech was kept at a minimum and the message of the rite was expressed in movement and gesture, touch and smile.

These ways of doing ordinary Chaplaincy things, the stock-in-trade of the job, took on a particular significance in the light of my relationship to the institution and its philosophy. Directness, lack of fuss, refusal to be professionally self-important or to take on an identity which belonged less to the job than to the institutional circumstances in which it was carried out—all these things reflected the church's judgment, not on the hospital itself, but on some of its attitudes and what they implied in the way of the triumph of systems over persons, both divine and human. In the highly organized world of the hospital, the result was definitely clownish, a paradoxical juxtaposition of setting and event, as when, sitting in a circle on the floor of the psychiatric clinic, the Chaplain and half a dozen other fools re-present the redemption of the world.

But the Chaplain has responsibilities outside as well as inside the hospital. He—or she—is under obedience to the ecclesiastical authority that ordained him or her, as well as to the wider church to which he or she belongs. For chaplains this has become a crucial role, as hospitals like Western Meads prepare to close down and to send their patients out into the community. Will the women and men who have attended the hospital chapel Sunday after Sunday, year upon year, manage to make contact with a local church that will welcome them and keep an eye on their progress? Will neighborly love be shown to the newcomers who move into the parish, whether or not they are used to coming to church? The churches with their parish and district networks provide an obvious means of establishing people in one kind of social belonging. A lonely ex-patient could be greatly helped and comforted by making contact with a friendly congregation.

As visiting preacher or lecturer to church groups, I have spent a great deal of time trying to prepare Christian congregations of various denominations for a closer involvement with people from Western Meads. I have to admit that I have not had much success. Churchgoers, like other people, are anxious about the unknown—which in this case is taken to be a great flood of ex-patients unleashed upon them, as the asylum voids itself upon the neighborhood. This has not happened, yet, of course. But it *might*. In some places, the rumor has it, it has already taken place with a disastrous effect upon property values. Property values, however, are not the immediate consideration, which is the terrifying prospect of living in close contact with one of them. This is not something to be dismissed lightly.

The Christian Church is well aware of its obligations towards social rejects: 'Insofar as ye did it unto one of these my little ones, ye did it unto me.' I can't help feeling that Jesus might well have had a word to say on the matter. The local church's reaction to the crisis was defensive, to say the least. Discussion often founders on the statement 'you can't expect the church to do the job that the government should be doing—if we help ex-patients, the authorities won't!' In an effort to dig deeper I sent a short questionnaire around to fifty local Anglican clergyman to see if they would welcome an opportunity to state their views away from the danger of face-to-face confrontation. I was surprised by the results. I sent fifty questionnaires out and got fifteen back, a reasonably high percentage for unsolicited material of this kind. The first question was 'what do you think the Church's response should be to hospital closure?' Nine replies stressed the responsibility of the government:

> . . . an ill-conceived plan . . .

> . . . the state took over welfare, health and education provision from the church over the last 150 years—it would be quite inappropriate for the church to accept it back . . .

> . . . the response should be pressure on the government For proper community support . . .

The Chaplains' Association should protest most strongly about the closure of hospitals.

Five clergy stressed the need for greater church involvement

> . . . the General Synod Board for Social Responsibility should be involved . . .

> . . . we should make representations to the government that adequate facilities within the community are available . . .

> . . . clergy and congregations should be equipped to meet the new situation . . .

> . . . a list of 'experts' at diocesan level . . .

Some replies stressed the responsibility of congregations to come to terms with the situation as it is at present, making the best of a bad job; four clergyman left this question unanswered; perhaps they couldn't trust themselves to reply!

The second question, concerning the church's response at the local level, achieved a higher level of agreement. Everybody who replied thought that something should, and could, be done, usually by themselves rather than other people. The idea of training courses for both clergy and laity came up several times, once within the context of interdenominational support groups, and plans for visiting newcomers to the parish were also mentioned. Most of the comment tended to be abstract, with frequent mention of 'caring' and 'compassion.' Two respondents wanted to see local organization for the kind of political action they were urging in answer to question one.

Finally, question three inquired about the reaction of congregations to the presence of ex-patients in their midst. Here there was almost complete unanimity: 'welcome', 'caring—no hassle,' 'O.K.' Four clergy, however, were not quite so sure—'some wariness,' 'probably just like their reaction to everyone else. Some would welcome them, others ignore them'—a reassuringly honest answer. Perhaps ordinariness is most important of all! None of the clergy claimed to know much about mental illness, although fourteen out of fifteen had come into contact with people suffering from it during the course of their pastoral duties; all fifteen said that they would like to know more. Altogether the picture seemed brighter than I had thought.

The attitude of these clergy did much to make me feel more hopeful about the future. There was little doubt that this hospital, along with all those like it, would not be with us much longer—four or five years at most. The huge organism, with its many parts and divisions, separate and yet connected, continuing care, rehabilitation, acute assessment, so many wards and departments, would be nothing more than a pathetic collection of useless buildings. Resurrection, when it comes, will be in another place and take a different form. I believe that the church will play its part in witnessing to this new birth.

(In fact the hospital had closed by the mid-1990s.)

5 FINDING THE WAY HOME

The hospital was home to many different kinds of people. I realized very soon that not all the patients were suffering from mental illness. Some had been ill when they were admitted and were not ill any longer. This was an obvious fact amongst those who had been in hospital for a long time. The most striking thing about most of the patients, the thing that visitors drew attention to, was their 'absence of psychiatric symptoms'—'What's wrong with *him*?' '*She* seems perfectly normal!' It became harder to make this kind of judgment with any accuracy because the growing effectiveness of psychiatric medication means that patients were usually seen 'at their best' when they were behaving, and feeling, like anybody else.

On the other hand, the visitor's remarks were just as relevant to them as to those hospital residents who were not receiving major medication of any kind because they were now too well to need it—if their treatment was so effective here in hospital, why couldn't it look after them outside? The hospital had so many long-stay patients, some of whom with symptoms that were controllable, others without symptoms of any kind. Why was this?

The main reason was to be found in the social role that the Meads had played over the years as a kind of repository for distressed and emotionally disabled people of all kinds. Anyone who was homeless and unable to fend for him or herself tended towards Western Meads.

Once here, they tended to stay. To call the Meads a dumping place, a social dustbin, is probably to overstate the case, but the fact is that the hospital was the refuge for all sorts of desperate, socially rejected and despised people who had nowhere else to go. This is far from being the intention of its founders, and was never really accepted as official policy by its medical staff. But once the poor houses were closed down, there was literally nowhere else for such people to go. The tradition of caring for homeless people continued into this century and was seen most strikingly in the hospital's reluctance to turn people out once they had recovered. It might take several months, or even years, for people who had once been ill to get well enough to leave, by which time the Meads had become their home, frequently referred to by them as such.

Harold's father died when he was twelve years old. This was a great loss, because he had never really known his mother, who had been knocked down by a car and killed while he and his sisters were still small children. That it was not a total tragedy was due to Harold's own strength of character and the way in which he rose to the challenge of his new role as head of the family. In some ways the desperate nature of the situation that he and his sisters found themselves in actually helped Harold to cope. He felt that he must concentrate every bit of strength he possessed on the task of looking after his three sisters because they were all he had left. The three little girls, who were seven, eight and ten years old, certainly pulled their weight in the little family and gave him a good deal of support. A bachelor uncle saw to the ways in which the finances were organized and the family next door kept a friendly eye on things (until the husband too suffered an accident and their attention turned away), while Harold and the girls saw to the division of labor within their own household.

It was not easy, having to go to school and run a house at the same time, but other people had done it before him and he was determined to do it too—he had his father to think about. And there was his mother, too, of course. He couldn't really remember his mother, except as a vague presence, a sad kind of sweetness he didn't think about very often because it made him want to cry, which he couldn't do for fear his sisters might see him. Now and again, when he was in his bedroom by himself—or on the lavatory—he was taken by surprise, the warm feeling came over him and he wept. Then he had to wash his face so that nobody would notice his swollen eyes. In the table in the bedroom there was a drawer with things in it. Some of these were things of his own that he had kept because, when he was young enough to play with them, she had still been there. Some had been given him by his father to remember her by.

He could remember most things about his father, however, even to the extent of going in the ambulance with him when he had to go to the hospital for the last time. He could remember the hospital ward, the way the door handles were polished, the different nurses' belts and badges, the strange taps you turned on and off with the back of your hand to stop the germs being spread around. Most of all, he remembered how his father had looked up at him from the bed where they had put him—looked at him as if he were a man, not a boy, treating him as an equal. Harold often thought of this and it gave him strength, made him feel more equal to facing up to all the things that lay ahead for him. It was as if his father was closer than he had ever been before, his friend rather than his parent, an ally in the struggle with life. From now on he modeled himself more or less consciously on him, as he set about trying to provide his sisters with the parent they had lost. It was not an easy thing to do and involved saying goodbye to childhood years before anybody should have to. There were so many things he would have liked to do, things everyone takes for granted, like school trips and bicycle rides or just wandering along the canal bank, which would have to be given up—and what would he have done when everyone else had got girl-friends?

That would come later, however. For the time being it was better to cross each bridge separately. The first thing was the girls. Harold got down to the practical details concerning their welfare. After a bit he found himself enjoying his new responsibilities. June, the eldest, was most difficult to get on with. She didn't see how a boy could do a grown-up's job, and she didn't hesitate to say so. Who did Harold think he was? He was only a couple of years older than her in any case! She tried to persuade her sisters, Christine and Valerie, not to co-operate with their conceited brother and for a few months life was extremely difficult. As he went about his greatly increased duties in the house, Harold found himself talking to his father out loud and this worried him too. 'I think you're going barmy,' said June.

Harold wasn't going mad, of course. He simply needed all the help he could get and not very much was forthcoming at that time from inside the family, although the two younger girls were never so resentful of his authority as their sister continued to be. The bachelor uncle did his best to help but he lived several miles away and never seemed to know what to do when he came over anyway. The adult members of the family next door popped in each day, but kept aloof from whatever was going on among the children, believing that it was their duty to 'avoid being drawn into quarrels.' So Harold continued to do the job more or less alone, aided only by his strong sense of purpose and the intermittent support and co-operation of his sisters.

A few miles away, in the no-man's land between villages, lived a maiden aunt, sister of Harold's mother. This lady, Auntie Dee, suffered badly from arthritis. Once a week Harold, Christine and Valerie went over to Auntie Dee's for what amounted to a change of housework and errands, although they enjoyed the walk. Harold was grateful for Auntie Dee because she seemed to be more on the girls' wavelength than he was. Sometimes they would want to stay the night and go to school next morning from Auntie Dee's house— it was further to walk but quite possible—and Harold would find himself trudging home through the dusk to an empty house. Miners, on their way to and from the pub, saw his small form striding out down the lane and wondered, again, how he was coping.

This was a mining community and had the strong sense of solidarity characteristic of such places. The neighbors did all sorts of things to help Harold and his sisters keep their heads above water, taking them to the seaside for day trips and on one occasion for a whole week's holiday at Skegness. (This was where the Postmistress always went. This time she said that she fancied company and took Harold and the girls along with her. Harold never forgot this holiday. He saved Valerie from drowning and, when he got home, he found himself a kind of village hero.)

As soon as he was old enough, Harold got a job in the pit. This was the happiest time of his life. Now he was earning a wage he really felt like the man of the house. His new status provided a satisfactory way of keeping his sisters under control. Now that the money was not simply administered by him but actually provided, earned by hard slogging away underground, there was a greater sense of belonging together. Just as Harold felt more like a real father, so June, Valerie and Christine began to feel maternal towards him. (Scrubbing someone's back gives rise to emotions of this kind.) However. it was not to last.

Everybody was growing up, of course, not only Harold. Valerie was the first to announce she was going to get married. She had a job as a dentist's receptionist in a nearby town. Harold couldn't understand why she wanted to give it up and leave home. He tried to reason with her, pointing out that they were a very special kind of family, not just an ordinary one: they had looked after one another all these years and been through all kinds of things together—this, surely made them special? She didn't want to be the first to break the family up, did she? Valerie burst into tears and promptly married her boyfriend, followed, five years later, by Christine. June was the last to go, and the hardest for Harold to say goodbye to. It was a good thing that everyone else was at the Miner's Institute getting the food ready. Nobody likes to see a collier weep.

This was the beginning of a very bad time for Harold, who became depressed in a way he had never known before and couldn't shake off. Eventually after several months he reached what seemed to be the point of no return. Life was unbearable now without his special family, the one he had created all on his own. He imagined a future which was totally black, just day after day of heaving coal with no-one to go back home to, no-one to hand the paypacket over to, no-one to love. What was it all for? What had it ever been for? No-one could pretend, not even the Coal Board, that slaving away in the dark was worth doing for its own sake! His mates tried to cheer him up, but it wasn't any use. They were good mates and he had always enjoyed their company, had enjoyed working alongside them, but they all had their families, whereas he had nobody. He had always been one for living in the present. His life had made him like that, one thing at a time. The fact was that he had never really thought they would go. Not *all* of them, not like that. He knew where they were, of course, and they came over to see him, bringing their husbands with them. Even Valerie, once she had got over her resentment at his 'selfishness,' used to come and visit him at least once a month, if she could manage it.

But it wasn't the same, not the same at all. It was no good pretending that it ever could be now. For Harold life was over. He went down to the canal side where he used to go when he was a boy on those occasions when life was particularly desolate and he had to be alone and try and find some kind of an answer. Only this time he couldn't find any answer. Fortunately a couple were kissing goodnight in the shade of the trees and heard the splash. Instead of running away down the towpath, they came to see what the noise was and dragged him out. The police were summoned and Harold was taken along to the emergency department of a nearby hospital. June was informed of what had happened and she and her husband arrived, in some distress, to take charge of things. Two days later Harold was taken to see a psychiatrist . . .

Which is how Harold came to take up residence in the psychiatric hospital. This, of course, was in the 1930s; he was thirty years old when it happened and he lived here, in the hospital, for forty years—until he was seventy. In those days, people who were considered to be, in the official phrase, 'a danger to themselves or others,' were kept secure until it was considered to be safe to let them out. Certainly, Harold was no danger to anyone else, but he had tried to kill himself. What he had done once, he might do again. Because it was difficult to control the symptoms of mental illness, and because some mental illnesses tend to recur, many patients spent a very long time in hospital in those days.

Harold had no family to return to, no-one at least who was willing to shoulder the responsibility of looking after someone who had been 'in that place.' Perhaps Harold preferred to stay in hospital rather than be a burden to his newly married sisters and their husbands, but I do not think he was given the option—here he was and here he was going to have to stay. Medical and nursing staff were very protective, very *custodial*, in those days, partly because people outside hospital were even more cruelly rejecting than they are now and partly because a tightly organized, rigidly stratified system of segregation and its accompanying chain of command was considered necessary in order to control the large numbers of patients committed to institutions like this one.

This, then, is the kind of environment in which Harold spent forty years of his life, fifteen years of which I knew him quite well. I don't believe he ever became resigned to being in hospital and he often complained to me about having to stay. When he was feeling 'down'—as they say here—he imagined some kind of plot against him on the part of the hospital to deprive him of his liberty. Imagining plots is a well-known symptom of paranoid schizophrenia, but it's difficult to see how you avoid it if you're in the position of someone like Harold. The fact is, he did become depressed from time to time and this seemed a good reason for keeping him in hospital, particularly as he had no home to go back to. When he was well, which was most of the time, there didn't seem to be the slightest excuse for his being here. The ward he lived on was the least restricted and institutional of any in the hospital, more like an old people's home than a psychiatric ward, and he lived among us as a neighbor rather than an asylum inmate. He was a regular member of the chapel congregation and one of the founders of the bible class. People, even staff members, asked his advice about things. He was respected by everyone, and by some quietly loved.

Harold's dilemma was a common one for psychiatric patients. You could call it a kind of self-fulfilling prophecy. He foresaw that he would be kept in hospital for the rest of his life and the prospect terrified him. Helped by his anti-depressant medication, he was able to put the idea out of his mind for long periods of time, but sooner or later the full force of his predicament would hit him and he became dreadfully depressed again. There was certainly not any possibility of asking his sisters for help. He still felt hurt at being abandoned all those years ago, when they left him alone. He knew very well that he had no reason to feel this; they had simply grown up and got married, which was really the best thing that could have happened, wasn't it? He was ashamed of the resentment he felt towards people he loved so much and it made him more depressed than ever. The psychiatrist in whose charge he was maintained that Harold's depression was an illness, probably inherited. Harold showed signs of the extreme variations in mood, swinging between cheerfulness and despair, which characterize manic-depression. This was a mild form, of course; one could hardly describe Harold's happier periods as 'mania.' But the principle was the same. When all was said and done, Harold was a patient and had been one for a long time.

Psychiatric hospitals tend to look different from the inside than the outside. An outsider might suppose that being incarcerated for year after year in a hospital like this one would be likely, if not certain, to make a person depressed, just as seeing other people discharged— often people who seem more disturbed than oneself—without ever managing to get anyone in authority to consider letting *you* go might well induce the symptoms of paranoia. From the hospital point of view, however, it is important to be able to say you were like this before you arrived, that you are in hospital because it is the most convenient place or because there really isn't anywhere else for you to go; these may be good reasons, but they aren't medical ones. If you are going to stay in a place like this you're going to need your label—which means that you have to go along with a doctor's way of describing your behavior. This is not difficult, because he or she will accept nonconformist behavior as evidence supporting the diagnosis—indeed your refusal to see yourself as ill is taken as convincing proof that you *are* ill, simply because really ill people lack the insight to know it!

I'm not saying that psychiatrists are always wrong when they diagnose people as having a mental illness. Sometimes they are, sometimes not. In a mental hospital, however, they tend to be always right. The defensive attitude described earlier contributes to this attitude of mind. The hospital is seen, and sees itself, as a place where an intractable problem is dealt with by specialists. This is obviously true of all hospitals, but it is more true of a psychiatric than of a general hospital, because psychiatric illnesses always involve at some point or another a breakdown in personal relationships. Physical illness may have the same kind of effect, as the pain and frustration suffered by sick people puts a tremendous strain on their ability to remain as cheerful and relaxed with others as they would like to do; the strain works both ways, as those who look after such relatives over a long period of time are only too aware. Whereas this is a burden laid upon a relationship, with psychiatric illness it is *the relationship itself* which seems to be sick. What happens between people in such situations seems to have the power to interfere with, or even in some cases, remove the possibility of any kind of normal relationship—normal, that is, in the sense of a common understanding of what is actually going on between people who used to get on well, or at least well enough.

This is a very disturbing thing to happen within any social group. When it occurs within families people are bewildered because they don't know what to do and are often extremely frightened. The old landmarks, habitual ways of talking and behaving, things that refer to years of sharing experiences, memories, attitudes of mind, appear to have disappeared, or somehow to have been shifted out of focus, so that people don't seem to be on the same wavelength any more. The usual reaction to this is to feel guilty because of a very deep-seated conviction that if we cannot communicate with someone we love it must be our fault; to feel *for* someone involves feeling *with* them and we are obliged at least to try to do this. Fear and guilt are not the only factors involved, but they dictate the tone of much psychiatric illness, because relationship itself depends on the courage to trust and a broken one leaves us questioning our own adequacy as people, which is both shameful and terrifying.

The hospital exists as a way of coping with impossible situations by bracketing them from ordinary life. Harold could not possibly cope. It was this consideration that bracketed him with manic depression and schizophrenia in the only available place. Diagnosis was really irrelevant, except as a means of getting people in. Everyone knows how variable psychiatric diagnosis is anyway. Once in, however, you were a patient—no doubt about that. Here, in this monstrous building, questions about mental illness found a definitive answer. The attitude of society has always been in favor of letting psychiatrists get on with trying to solve a problem nobody can deal with, one which because of its nature gives rise to widespread public distaste and panic among those personally involved. Unfortunately, where only one interpretation of a state of affairs was allowed, those who supported it could act much as they saw fit. If Harold had taken upon himself to disagree with the official view of the situation, he would have found scant success in the very place where the doctors' authority was concentrated, the hospital specifically set apart from society for psychiatry to practice the arts which it alone understood. He didn't of course. It was not for him to 'fly over the Cuckoo's nest!'

Instead, Harold did other things to express his individuality. They were not so dramatic as protest or rebellion (nor as futile as such things always turned out to be in these circumstances). Before coming into hospital he spent all his life looking after other people and this is what he did here. The staff remember him with a good deal of warmth because of his kindness to other patients. We used to hold a weekly bible study on his ward and Harold was one of those who always came to it. In fact, he sometimes led it, because leading worship was one of the things he did best. Harold was a great help to the church here. He had never actually become a Lay Reader—he had never, with all his responsibilities, had the time to concentrate on any kind of systematic studying. However, he, and his sisters, had regularly attended the Parish Church. Indeed, during the last few years before the family finally broke up, they had sung together in the church choir. At first this was only Harold, who had been a member since he was seven years old; once established in his role as head of the household, he was able to enrol all three sisters. This gave him a tremendous amount of satisfaction and he often used to talk about it in the years he spent in hospital.

When we knew him. Harold had a pleasant tenor voice, a little shaky on the high notes, particularly if it was music he loved, and that moved him. As may be imagined this was a great asset to the worship in the hospital chapel, particularly when he was singing solo, which he was delighted to be asked to do, but exceedingly shy about doing. By the time I came to the hospital as Chaplain, the chapel services had begun to change from a very traditional Prayer Book Matins and Holy Communion to the modern English Rite A of the Alternative Service Book. Most of the congregation seemed to adjust readily enough, being used to having to do what they were told, even in church. Besides, the new service was more lively and you didn't have to leave half-way through if you weren't confirmed, which was a great advantage.

Harold thought otherwise. It was hard to persuade him to come to church at all, let alone sing. What had happened to his beloved psalter—the Anglican chant on which he had been brought up, and which his father had sung so splendidly in the choir stalls of the village church? This was no trivial matter. The chapel was the most important place in the hospital for him. Its presence at the corner of the grounds focussed all his hopes and aspirations. Its services expressed everything he had held to be most precious, during his whole life. Indeed the chapel held his life together. It was his link with normality as well as with God. It was the one thing that had not changed and he thanked God for it. He didn't see any reason to pretend that he was happy with what was going on. This was certainly a hard time for him and his loyalty was decidedly strained. We were all very relieved when he accepted the new *status quo* and began to sing solos again, as if nothing had happened.

Then, quite suddenly, something did happen. Something amazing. Valerie, who had emigrated to New Zealand in the 1960s, invited Harold to go out and live with her. Her husband had died and she felt she would like to make life a bit more pleasant for her brother. Christine had already joined her. In fact she had been out there for several years. Harold had been out on two occasions to spend Christmas in New Zealand but his time over there had been restricted to a few weeks. The idea of going out for good had remained a kind of fantasy, something never seriously discussed. He was seventy years old and people thought that was too old to start a new life. Harold said he would love to have gone, but it was quite impossible. Besides, he hadn't been asked. He went on to point out that the hospital would never give him a clean bill of health. I thought he was probably right about this at least. I also wondered about the attitude of the New Zealand immigration authorities towards people who had lived in a psychiatric hospital for forty years. It was a marvelous plan—but how could it ever be put into operation? When you thought about it, it was a bit cruel to have suggested it! Didn't Valerie know the difficulties involved?

Valerie did know and had already taken steps to overcome the most important ones. First of all she wrote to the Hospital Secretary asking for his help in what she intended to do. A kindly man, he would certainly do all he could to convince the authorities of Harold's suitability as a new resident in their country. Secondly, Valerie got in touch with me, as Harold's friend and Chaplain of the Hospital. I let them know that for Harold's sake I was happy about the opportunity he had had to leave us, but very sorry to see him go. He had been a pillar of my congregation and the hospital would be the poorer without his presence. Most important of all was the fact that, during his last visit, Harold had been taken to see a psychiatrist in New Zealand, who had declared him to be perfectly well. His psychiatrist at the hospital was not willing to commit himself on this point and this would normally have been quite enough to prevent his going, but the immigration and health authorities in New Zealand preferred the local opinion and gave permission for Harold to set about making his preparations and saying his goodbyes.

This is more or less the end of this story except to say that he continued to be well and lived happily in New Zealand. In a letter at the time this book was originally written, Harold said that he now had his own house, next door to the one where Valerie and Christine live. He went swimming with them at Christmas and the three went on holiday together. I have a marvelous letter that Harold wrote about a trip to Hawaii. He went among the islands in a glass-bottomed boat and he described the colors of the fish darting over the coral. It all seemed a world away from here. (I don't think Harold is still alive. Some time during the last twenty years we lost touch.)

Harold's story tells of his deep love for his sisters and how that love was dramatically returned. It is really a story about love. In the same way Harold's years in hospital were characterized by all kinds of love, not least the love he shared with us in the hospital church. It all adds up to an account of the vicissitudes of loving.

Here we must stop, however, before we try to carry this argument further and fall into the trap of trying to think up some kind of list of positive aspects belonging to depression itself. We may as well admit here and now that there aren't any. Depression has no fringe benefits. It is a dead weight. I say 'dead' because this is what it is. It has been said that depression is a foretaste of death, death as a wholly negative experience, the negation of experience. You can't live in it, so you can't learn from it, which means you can't prepare for it. For anyone with faith in God, this may actually present itself as worse than dying, for dying holds out the hope of a life which is more real, more genuine than this. This death, however, has no such hope. Indeed, while it lasts, it has no hope of any kind. The ordinary things of life, the things we take for granted as evidence of an over- all goodness and rightness of creation, no longer have any power to comfort us. It is as if there has been a species of 'world-swap,' a drastic change in the kind of thing we are able to feel, reflected in what we are able to feel it about. In fact, of course, this is what has actually happened. The mirror of the mind, upon which all the events and presences of life are reflected, is turned in on itself, away from its true business of exploring the universe of people and things, back towards its own painful preoccupations and frustrated desires. We remain shut up in a dungeon of our own making.

Or this is how it seems to us. Thinking is no longer any good at all; we have done too much of it. Nothing is immediate, nothing is vivid, nothing is real. We ourselves are no longer real, despite all our efforts to grasp our own reality by concentrating so hard on what it is that is going on inside ourselves. We discover to our cost that simply grasping after being is not enough to enable us to be. We revisit the places we loved, listen to the music that filled us with rapture, turn in desperation to the poems which always used to speak so personally to us. None of this works any more; we can't believe it ever did.

There was a lot of this about at Western Meads. From time to time I used to fall into the condition myself. I would gaze at the prison- like buildings and weep. What had I done to end up in such a place? Whatever it was, I had done it myself, *to* myself . . . At such times, I could hardly bear to look at people. I know now that I was suffering from depression because the effect of this kind of intractable sadness upon the sufferer's experience of other people is the most striking symptom of all. Because of the unique nature of human relationship, in which experiences of all kinds are reflected backwards and forwards, people suffering from this kind of self-imprisonment are acutely aware of the effects of their own pain upon others. They can no longer receive the healing joy of another's love while the anguish they themselves feel is only too readily internalized by those who want—who need—to help them. The responsiveness which is human relationship is always a two-way process; we do not simply give to the world, nor do we receive from it. We are *in communion* with it. When the interchange of being breaks down, we look to ourselves to see whether we have played our part properly, have given enough to the relationship to preserve its mutuality. And if we haven't—or if we think we haven't—we hold ourselves responsible.

I believe that the guilt of depression is connected to this. Whatever its neurological correlates may be, it is the guilt of frustration, the profound existential frustration which comes from inability to respond to love. In a way it is a sign of love, because it expresses a profound need for reconciliation with other people and with life itself. It longs for reconciliation with belonging, for reconciliation with God. You could say that the depressive's sense of guilt is an extreme awareness of the alienation we call sin. You could also say that he or she senses the fact more powerfully, more painfully, than the rest of us do.

I am not talking about sin in connection with depressed people at Western Meads because of their special sinfulness, but because the weight of depression bearing down upon the hospital, and others like it, seems to invite discussion. It could be said that depressed people bear our sins, because they have been brought into contact with the origin of sin, the breakdown of the primal relationship between self and other and because, in a way and to an extent that escapes other people, they take on the responsibility for being human. As far as a sense of sin goes, depressed people carry a load far greater than the rest of us, a load which seems to be out of all relationship with their

81

own personal guilt. They do not see it this way. They believe that they deserve everything that is happening to them, and much more as well. Nor do they blame God for their misfortune as others are tempted to do for that would be to some extent to excuse themselves, which is precisely what they cannot ever do. There is no escape from the guilt which holds them fast, which is both the jail and the jailer, as it is also Judge and Jury, prosecuting attorney and even hangman. This guilt is both subjective and objective: what they do and what they are. The attempt to see beyond it only reinforces its presence. How can it do otherwise when looking itself is guilty?

You cannot lift yourself out of this quagmire. You have to be rescued. One way, the way that is commonly used, is by modifying the chemistry of the brain to make it less sluggish, more receptive to stimulation, more open to whatever is going on outside itself. Mental processes are speeded up by antidepressant drugs, and with them the mechanisms involved in interpersonal relationship helped to function in a livelier manner. This kind of approach is widely used and we should thank God for the scientific expertise that has made it available. It must be pointed out, however, that it depends for its success on events which take place outside the brain as much as biochemical changes inside it. In other words, there must be people one can relate to, people who are able and willing to come forward in friendship and love so that links with the outside world may be restored on a basis of common understanding and mutual support. This is true of ideas as well as people. If, after the sheer weight of depression has been lifted by chemical means, we can see no hope of any kind for ourselves, because nothing has changed within our personal environment, then we are likely to lapse again into depression. Now that we can see what it was that made us depressed, there seems little point in having got better. When I was depressed, I could only see myself and my unique agony. Now, I can see more than I can bear to see.

I have said that the guilt of depression is the failure of our responsibility to see what has to be seen. We have a responsibility to live with reality, our own and other people's. In depression we shut down on ourselves, building a prison we cannot bear to live in, the prison of our own refusal to take account of the reality confronting us. It seems to me that this represents a vulnerability which belongs to our nature as human beings; there is only so much we can bear without turning in on ourselves. The guilt we feel is one we cannot help feeling; it is the measure of an instinctive awareness of our responsibility to others, and consequently to ourselves. For we belong together and can only live as ourselves in the interchange of relationship. If it is real guilt, this is because we are really human, really sinners. We are rescued from it by love, the love of God communicated in countless ways but most noticeably in the ordinary life of relationship. This was Harold's life, the presence that sustained him during his years in hospital. This life was both his prize and his gift, encouraging others in the captivity of their illness, being encouraged by others when times were particularly hard for him.

He had lost both home and family. Two of his sisters had gone where he could never join them—at least, that is what he believed—and it certainly seemed unlikely, even impossible, that he would ever be able to do so. His other sister seemed to have vanished altogether; she neither wrote to him nor came to see him and his letters to her were unanswered. The Harold of those former days, valiant provider for the small family for which he acted as surrogate father and mother, keeping alive the trust laid on him by his dead parents—this person had also ceased to exist. In place was an aging mental patient, confirmed in inferiority by the discipline of a hospital ward and stigmatized as a mental patient by the all too obvious illness of the people who surrounded him. We should not be surprised that from to time he became depressed. What is more remarkable is that this only happened comparatively rarely. Most of the time Harold cared for others the way he had looked after his own family. Certainly there was something keeping him going all those years. Something, or someone.

The drama of Christ's death and resurrection is present in commonplace stories like this. In Harold's case the second act has been extended to almost thirty years, the time spent in hospital between the breakdown of the family and Harold's departure for a new life in New Zealand. But this is the most important part of the story, the part that divides death from resurrection and reveals the nature of both. This is the descent into hell, the in-between where nothing has actually finished nor properly begun, so that people are neither what they were nor what they will eventually be, where nothing is really anything at all, but everything reaches out to find itself in an endless, or seemingly endless, search for meaning and value.

Because it concentrates on the central point of change, spelling out the endless moments between death and life, Harold's story is a particularly clear illustration of the way Christians believe that God works in the world, the way of death and resurrection. I have suggested that Harold was helped during his years in hospital by the presence of God. At every stage of the journey God was with him, not as a fellow traveler only, but as the journey itself, because of the shape of Harold's story, the resurrection-shape of God's revelation. God is not a character in it, someone at work 'in' or 'behind' it, but actually *is* for us the story. It is through resurrection events like this that God becomes present to us and we recognize him in the meaning we are able to give to the relationship of ordinary events. Our involvement with the divine is the same as our involvement with the things that happen to us in the world, for the way things 'hang together' cannot help suggesting the conclusions we draw from them. God is, for us, *the journey through death into life*.

So, as well as being the experience of involvement, the meaning of our joy and pain, God is also the story of our journeying. Again, it seems strange to be talking about journeys in such a context. What kind of a journey is anyone making when they are incarcerated in a mental hospital for thirty years? Obviously one that extends beyond the present moment to seize upon the real meaning of what is happening now. However boring and uneventful it may be, the present has power to organize past and future into a story we can live with. 'Stone walls do not a prison make, Nor iron bars a cage.' Most of the time Harold could look beyond Western Meads and rejoice in the life that his sisters were enjoying because of the care he had bestowed on them. Apart from the times when he could not distinguish any kind of sense at all, he could see the purpose of his life very clearly indeed, as he read and re-read the letters that arrived regularly from New Zealand and made a strange kind of sense of his loneliness—'if you take the broad view, Roger.'

6 FOUR MORE JOURNEYS

Looking over what I have written about Western Meads I have to say that I'm not very happy about it. I wanted to describe the kind of thing that goes on there as accurately as I could. I don't know whether I've managed to do that or not, but I've certainly failed to make the place come to life in the way I had hoped that it would. I suppose that I was trying to counter-balance the account I gave of Hillside, which was written from the most painful personal memories and couldn't really be set down in any other way. I wanted Western Meads to reflect my changed attitudes and opinions about myself and other people and—more importantly—the difference in my relationship with the hospital. I wanted to show how different being a staff member was from being a patient.

But I also want 'the Meads' to speak for itself. I want you to get the feel of the place, which you are unlikely to do from this kind of description, or only with great difficulty, looking beyond the rather forbidding and institutional exterior to catch a glimpse of the life going on inside. No-one would even want to visit Western Meads from my description of it, never mind live there. And yet there are some people for whom it means something quite different, for whom it is actually home, as passionately hated and sincerely loved as only home can be. Some of these people are staff, some patients. They are usually people who have found love here, forcing its way up like a flower between paving stones, humanizing the grimness of the old hospital and transforming its nature more radically than any Mental Health Act could ever do.

Tony had lived in the hospital for a long time. He was an orphan and had spent his first few years in a children's home. A tendency to 'interfere' with children younger than himself led to his incarceration in the county asylum while still in his early teens. There were not many people of his age in the place when he arrived; the general opinion was that this was a good thing. One other person left the orphanage at the same time in order to take up residence in the grim Victorian buildings. So far as personality went, Jane had little in common with Tony. Whereas he was quiet and withdrawn, tentative in his relationships with other people, eager to please and anxious to avoid trouble at any cost, Jane was a fiery creature with bright red hair, always in trouble because of a temper which she seemed never to be able to control. Jane was subject to epileptic fits. Whether these were triggered off by the outbursts of resentment which usually preceded them or the outbursts were a neurological advance warning for the fits, the result was precisely the same, and Jane spent many hours and days in seclusion. Meanwhile, Tony had attached himself to the hospital gardeners. When Autumn came round I used to see him busily at work on the mounds of sodden greenery which overflowed the gutters and made the pathways of the hospital dangerous to passers-by. It was a job he enjoyed doing, particularly when it involved lifting the cast-iron gratings and delving into the drainage system beneath the hospital. Even within the hospital, Tony's life was different from Jane's. He had found his way to a kind of freedom, exploring a world to which few, if any, had access, a network of pathways which meandered round the hospital, before penetrating into the depths in order to trace a circuitous route under the hospital before breaking out into the sunlight again.

At this time Tony's life was very different from Jane's. Even the physical presence of the hospital was different. If Tony's investigations had ever led him up the staircase which leads from the abandoned airing court at the South East corner of the old female block, he would not have been surprised to find it safely bricked up. There had been many changes since the main gates had been opened and the majority of patients made 'informal.' For Jane, things had not changed all that much, however. A few feet away from the bricked-up door she would be sitting huddled in her chair under the sternly custodial gaze of the ward staff, officially at liberty, yet not able to go anywhere, because her clothes would have been taken away from her. She would be very angry and on the edge of a fit.

These two, Jane and Tony, divided by an institution which divides them both from us, different in temperament and by psychiatric diagnosis, were to fall deeply in love. This in itself seems unlikely, as one of the pair, Tony, had always showed more interest in his own sex than the opposite one. There was no question of his devotion to Jane, however. This was not to be the kind of transient hospital romance which is such a feature of institutional life, particularly in psychiatric hospitals. Determined that it should last, they came along to see the hospital chaplain to see if they could get married.

I admit to having been taken aback. What were the rules about patients marrying each other? I had been here for several years and I was well aware that the hospital discouraged it, and for very good reasons, too. Patients are simply not well enough—otherwise they wouldn't be patients, would they? If both partners are patients, the situation is more than twice as bad because of the danger of their making each other worse. There is also the question about children; surely it would be irresponsible to sentence unborn children to life in a psychiatrically unstable environment. If one of the patients suffers from a hereditary illness, the situation is even more clear-cut; there is no way in which a doctor or a nurse could condone this. What would be the position with regard to Jane's epilepsy?

Finally, and perhaps more damningly than any of these—Tony and Jane could have had no inkling of the reality of what went on in the world outside the hospital. Inside the institution their needs were catered for with a minimum of effort on their part; every day was mapped out for them. They did not need to worry about any of the practical considerations which confront the rest of us at so many points in our lives—jobs, accommodation, pensions, insurance, available benefits, medical help of all kinds, the list was almost endless. The hospital had become their home; as long as they were capable of a basic response to or acknowledgment of another person they were assured of allies and friends within the institution. Certainly, Jane and Tony were never short of people to share things with during their years here. They knew who would listen to their complaints and comfort their distress, who was good for a fag or a game of billiards, or a chat about old times. They would find things very different 'on the outside.' It would be unfair to expect them to cope. They must somehow be guided away from a course of action which could well have tragic consequences.

In spite of this, however, Tony and Jane went ahead. The lady at the Citizen's Advice Bureau directed them first to a lawyer and then back to me. The lawyer told them that they were legally free to marry and I said I would marry them. At least, I said I would conduct a service of blessing in the hospital chapel when they returned from the Register Office. The chapel is not licensed for weddings and a civil ceremony seemed more suitable as we wanted to be as discreet as possible. I kept thinking that one of the two consultant psychiatrists concerned might change his mind and put a restraining order on the bride or the groom. It would be bad enough if the strain of the ceremony caused Jane to have an epileptic fit; if the wedding were actually canceled, heaven knows what the effect would be. But everything went well and I had the tremendous joy and privilege of giving the bride and groom Holy Communion. Sister on Jane's ward, who strongly disapproved, organized a splendid Wedding Breakfast. They left this hospital for the last time and set up house together, first of all in a bed-sit rented from a Sikh family, then in a council house on one of our local estates. Now and again I see them in the town when I go shopping. They both look very well. Tony can't get a job, of course, but he always looks very smart. Jane's fits are much less frequent.

Was I right to encourage them as I did? They were very much in love—so much was plain—but shouldn't I have been more sensible, more adult, paid more attention to all the things that stood in the way of such a marriage working, the pitfalls which lie in wait for those who embark on marriage even in the most propitious circumstances? From one point of view, I had no option of course. They were both of age—in their early twenties—and, as informal patients, legally free to marry. They would get married even if, as Jane said, they 'had to move heaven and earth' to do so. Would it have been better to have left the marriage un-blessed? As I say, I had no option. I could try to dissuade them by reminding them of all the things that were against such a marriage as theirs ever succeeding. Such was my duty, and I can report that I at least tried to carry it out.

I didn't do it very well, however. Somehow my heart wasn't in it. It wasn't only because I knew very well that my warnings would have absolutely no effect; it was something much more positive concerning Jane and Tony themselves. It was something about their love for one another. There was between these two a remarkable parity of concern, an interchange of loving sensitivity which I have rarely come across anywhere before or since. This was reflected in the delicacy of the respect in which they held one another when they were together. Nothing was expected of the other but love. Because neither was eager to take the lead in any decisions concerning both, there were endless arguments but little resentment and no serious quarrels. Never having learned 'appropriate social behavior' within a family, they had managed to avoid the sexual stereotypes that go with it. Neither was dominant nor submissive for longer than it took to gauge the effect produced on the other. Such attitudes were moves in an endless game in which the relationship was enjoyed for its own sake, not fixed roles in a rigidly plotted drama. This was a firm alliance, founded on a deep love and a degree of mutual respect I had not encountered before. Above all it was resilient, more resilient than I would have expected under the circumstances. How could this be?

Strange as it may seem, I believe that Tony and Jane had learned this way of relating in the hospital. Deprived of the normal models and the cultural assumptions embodied in them, they had looked elsewhere for guidance. Institutional rules had taught them how inflexible, not to say impersonal, the overall circumstances of our life together can be. There is no arguing with the authority of the institution and its officers. The relationships necessary for survival as a person must be sought elsewhere. The social life which exists among the patients within a large institution may be lacking in novelty and articulation but it is nevertheless a kind of corporate existence. The number of social roles in this society has very little to do with the way it is officially divided up—that is by the authorities who run the hospital and the professions functioning within it. As in a school, or a prisoner-of-war camp, alliances are made across all kinds of organizational boundaries. People who are attracted to each other through mutual interests soon establish contact. In such circumstances people who begin to find each other personally attractive have time to let the feelings grow and deepen as they wait for an opportunity to give their love free expression. And apart from all this, it is always wiser in such places to learn how to get on with people. After all, you're all in the same boat.

This kind of comradeship, the give and take of social life among the patient community, is what gave Jane and Tony's relationship its characteristic strength and flexibility. It is what permitted them to survive outside the hospital which had sheltered them for so many years. They had learned that, although you might have difficulties with 'the authorities,' you can usually trust people. At least, that is the presumption they make. Outside the hospital, the neighbors tended to find them amiable but annoying. They were used, they said, 'to live and let live,' but not to the strictness with which the rule, as interpreted by Jane and Tony, who always seemed surprised when they complained of the radio being on too loud when father was on late shift. The volume was immediately lowered and no offense taken—on the offenders' side at least. It was a different matter when the couple became really angry either with each other or someone else. On these occasions you could hear them shouting several streets away. However, it usually ended as abruptly as it began. Tony and Jane were not upset. After all, everyone gets angry, don't they? You always calm down after a bit. It doesn't mean anything, does it? And people tended to agree with them.

Jane and Tony managed to survive in their new surroundings because of three kinds of caring. The first kind was the powerful feeling of mutual identification, the quality of sharing, which was between them as a couple. As I said, this was a particularly useful kind of love for people in their position—imaginative and realistic, tender yet tough, born of a history of defeats and victories shared and survived. It was is if, having neither mother nor father they could remember, they had invented the roles and shared them out between themselves and then forgotten whose was which. This was useful in the necessity to cope with the unknown when the ability to improvise is the most important skill of all. The second kind of love reinforced the security of the first. There were many fathers and mothers, and uncles and aunts, for Tony and Jane here in the hospital, which functioned like a huge extended family, patients and staff thrown together by the business of caring for vulnerable people (patients *and* staff) and the necessity to maintain morale in the face of the universal stigma which attaches to hospitals like this one. The atmosphere in which these two were nurtured was one of 'bearing one another's burdens.' Sometimes the burden-bearing was rigorous and directive, sometimes it was supportive and indulgent, but it was always inspired by a genuine desire to care. In the years I worked there I was continually surprised by the fellow-feeling which existed not only among the patients themselves, but between patients and staff.

Things would be rather different outside the hospital, of course. People who were forced to abandon this kind of protective environment and found themselves in a position where they suddenly had to cope with an alien, frequently hostile, environment might well wish they had stayed at home. Even here, however, a disadvantage turned out to be an asset. Tony and Jane found that their very incompetence commended itself to their new neighbors. Owing to the circumstances of their rapid departure from the hospital, which had by-passed the ordinary rehabilitation procedures which led to the discharge of patients, Jane and Tony knew next to nothing of the everyday tasks which people take for granted. House-work, cooking, shopping, looking for a job, 'signing-on,' registering with a doctor were all, more or less, excursions into the unknown. They had been receiving psychiatric treatment for many years and could not break off now without ill effects; so a Community Psychiatric Nurse visited them from time to time. Apart from this tenuous link with the past Jane and Tony were on their own.

This is the crucial point of the story. At this juncture disaster could well have occurred, for it is at least doubtful whether the loving acceptance and understanding that they shared could have managed to keep them afloat in the troubled waters of the sea of prejudice which surrounds people who are known to have come into close contact with mental illness. Neighbors who refuse to answer when you say hello to them at the shops, who carefully cross over to the other side of the street when they see you approaching, who write letters about you to the Social Service Department, not because of anything you have done, but because of what, being you, you *might* do—this kind of thing makes life unbearable for anybody, particularly for those who set a high value on getting along with people and are accustomed to being generally liked and appreciated by their peers. This sort of treatment confused Tony and his bride a good deal when they first moved out of hospital. Gradually, confusion gave way to anger, turning them in on themselves, so that it was hard to persuade them out of the house at all. The volume went up on the radio, the quarrels became louder and more frequent, doors were slammed late at night.

And then, things began to change. Instead of simply knocking on the dividing well, one of the neighbors took the bit between her teeth and came in through the back door. Always polite, Jane invited her to sit down and Tony made her a mug of tea. It seemed that they didn't object to her intrusion. On the contrary, they were glad to see her, glad to have someone to talk to. As the weeks passed they saw her more often, and not only her, for she had lived in that street for a long time and had many friends who were quite willing to make contact with the newcomers once the ice had been broken. It seemed that people really wanted to help after all. Underneath their defensiveness was a sympathy which could quite easily develop into empathy, and then into a kind of love, the responsive love we feel towards those who are helpless and dependent—particularly if they are affectionate as well. This was the love that led to Jane's and Tony's survival. It was a special kind of love because it recognized the independence of the beloved. The newcomers were accepted as themselves. Instead of being deplored as something alien and terrifying their uniqueness was actually celebrated. The hard shell of prejudice was pierced and a surprising tenderness revealed itself.

The story illustrates several kinds of love—love that shares, love that trusts, love that enables, the love of partners, fellow sufferers, neighbors. All the same, I have reason to believe that there is a fundamental *way* of loving, one that is close to the very nature of love itself as men and women may experience it. This is the love that is fulfilled in letting-be, the creative movement of soul which came to the aid of Jane and Tony and gave them the ability to survive all the perils of a foreign land. It is a love that rests on solid foundations, for it is rooted in paradise, in that experience of total well-being which asks nothing of God but simple conformity to his will.

Until the apple attracted them Adam and Eve probably enjoyed God without thinking very much about their relationship with him. In other words, they loved him as they loved each other, each other in him and him in each other. The kind of relationship in which free selves move backwards and forwards in their contemplation of one another originated *after* the expulsion from Eden. This is the characteristic form of personal relationship, in which we remind ourselves of the other person, and of ourselves in relationship with them, by freely turning away from ourselves and towards them. Eve and Adam were certainly free in Eden, free to stay, and when the time came, free to listen to the being who embodied selfishness and to make their own decision about disobeying God. The freedom that had always been theirs as inheritors of the *imago dei* accompanied them across the threshold, but in a more mature form, characterized by increased self-consciousness, what the story describes as the knowledge of good and evil, the hall-mark of human awareness as we understand it to be in our own lives within the world. The origin of this ordinary human awareness is to be found in the blissful security of a perfect relationship of love with love, in which all personal satisfaction is found in and through the other. This is the biblical view of Eden, as it is a Christian's vision of heaven, the end of the story which perfectly balances the beginning. (Not only a Christian's, of course, for many religions share this picture of God's will for men and women.) We are entitled to ask whether the kind of relationship which bound Adam and Eve to God—and to each other—in Eden was yet fully human, fully personal, so long as they remained unaware of the extent of their own freedom—by which I mean their ability to offend Him. Could they distance themselves from the presence of glory to conceive of God's dignity and want to copy it? You can't sin if you don't know what sinning is. And if you can't sin, you can't really obey. Someone has to let you in on the secret, even if it's only a snake.

It would be stretching a point to regard any hospital as being just like the Garden of Eden. Even the most cunningly designed modern clinic, shaded by trees from sight of the main road, its discrete architecture reflected in the tranquil waters of a lake, holds within itself the suggestion of things we prefer not to think about. There are some things which are made more frightening by the attempt to play them down. At least that cannot be said about mental hospitals, whose purpose does not attempt to disguise itself so that they can be consequently used as agents of social control throughout entire neighborhoods and for miles around—wherever in fact an angry mother reaches for the appropriate threat with which to terrify a disobedient child. No need for *cherubim* here!

The hospital where Tony and Jane spent so many years is grimly uninviting, a place where many have known intolerable pain, and some still do, even today when the treatment for mental illness is so much more effective than it used to be. Yet its appearance, and certainly its reputation, are misleading. For Jane and Tony, as for many others, it was home. Certainly Tony was happier here than Jane, who spent many hours locked up in what was euphemistically called a 'side room.' But surprisingly enough, even Jane seemed to be fond of the place; she was certainly not eager to leave when the time came, and for more positive reasons than the fear of what might happen to her outside. She had a network of friends among the patients and staff of the hospital where she was a well-known personality, very much appreciated or her lively sense of humor. In a somewhat monochrome environment, with a good deal of regimentation so far as the daily routine was concerned, Jane's red hair shone like a beacon, directing interest to the point of greatest life, and consequently hope. 'If there's something going on here, you know who'll always be in the middle of it,' said a nurse and another said, 'when Jane left, a part of the hospital left with her.' Although not born there, Jane had an organic relationship to the social life of the hospital where she had lived since a child; what she lacked in the way of parents she made up for with a host of uncles and aunts and a supportively admiring peer group.

Later on, of course, there was Tony. Tony was not so salient a contributor to hospital life as Jane. What helped him to survive in that repressive world—repressive as far as the development of an independent personality was concerned—was his skill in adapting to changing circumstances over which he had little or no control. Tony was what is often called 'a born survivor,' although I have no doubt that this is something a person has to learn. It does not come automatically. Somehow, at some point, Tony had felt secure enough to commit himself to the enterprise of reaching out to his fellow human beings and to trust the outcome, however hazardous. It was an ability which he had developed consistently during his years in the hospital and people liked him for it and 'got on' with him. Those who thought that, to rate consideration as a human being you have to be awkward and quarrelsome, made the mistake of dismissing Tony; I have heard him described as 'unstable,' or even downright weak. I do not believe that this is the case. It certainly took strength of mind and purpose to quit the world he was so well adjusted to—more so than Jane perhaps—say goodbye to all his friends and walk out of the hospital that was his home and hers.

During the first months after the break had been made, my opinion of Tony's toughness rapidly grew, as I saw how he came to terms with life in a particularly cramped and squalid bed-sitter. He and Jane grew even closer together in their determination to succeed, in their bid for freedom and a new life together. I don't know for sure how they made it work, but the combination of Jane's energy and Tony's optimism kept them afloat until they were able to move where there were new friends to be made. Like Adam and Eve, they certainly had to work hard to keep alive in the world outside the gates.

Bert lives on Crofton ward. I shall write about him as if he were still there, all these years later, as I find it hard to think of him any other way. He has only been on this ward for a few months, but he has lived in the hospital for twenty five years, having spent twenty years in another psychiatric hospital prior to coming here. As far as Bert was concerned he has always been on the move. His life in the two hospitals has been a succession of minor upheavals reflecting alterations in official policy, the continual process of ward improvement or re-decoration, the process of ward closure and consequent re-deployment of patients. In ordinary human terms this means that men and women who have lived in a particular place long enough for it to become personal to them and have made friends they can really trust, undergo an experience as a result of which they are summarily deprived of both. This may not seem to be a very great hardship for those who never chose to come here in the first place and who loathe the hospital and themselves for being in it. Patients like this—and there are many of them—grow attached to their own personal environment of bed-space, shelf-unit, arm-chair and object strongly to having to exchange it for one that really belongs to someone else (even if your world consists of the particular corner of the 'day room' where Nurse sets you down on your bean-bag, you feel angry when it is suddenly a different corner in an alien room. I have been on wards which have just been re-settled in this way and felt the anger which hovers in the atmosphere—and not only among the patients!)

Bert, however, is different. Apart from the traumatic event of becoming a patient at his first hospital and the changes involved in leaving there and being transferred to this one, Bert has been forced to decamp dozens of times during the quarter century he has been at Western Meads. To him, however, each move is a challenge and an adventure. He is not simply used to changing wards; indeed it usually seems to come as a surprise to him, a welcome surprise because of the new opportunities it presents. For Bert each disruption of routine is the promise of a new lease of life, a time and place to glorify God. For Bert, ward exchanges are staging posts on the journey to broader acres.

His spiritual journey began sixty or so years ago in a town about ten miles away from the hospital. He belonged to a church-going family and attended first Sunday School, then choir, gaining a knowledge of the prayer book and psalter which has been with him ever since. His brother was already working down the pit and, as soon as he was old enough, Bert, too, became a collier. He does not seem to have objected to this; in that place, at that time, there was little else to do in the way of work. Bert has a cheerful disposition and makes his experiences sound quite exciting. It was dark down there in the pit, though, and he didn't like that: 'It was just black. It must've been a whole mile under the earth.' Perhaps it was the blackness that defeated him, the contrast between the coal-dust on his hands and the visionary brilliance within his mind led him to opt for the latter to the extent of denying the former's existence.

Anyway, Bert did not last long down the mine. Instead he went mad and was admitted to the first of his two psychiatric hospitals. I do not know the precise diagnosis, but the main symptom must have been joy. Bert's life is characterized by the tendency to see hope in every direction, coupled, it must be said, by a grasp of the facts which is not always as reliable as it might be. Both these tendencies are considered to be signs of insanity, the joy giving rise to more institutional discomposure than the disordered thought ever did. Three quarters of the time he is speaking to you Bert makes perfect sense; then, because he sees a connection you do not, or chooses to ignore a logical rule most people regard as essential, you have a powerful sense of having lost the thread somewhere and want to ask if you can start again and get it right this time.

Conversations of this kind are usually considered to be of clinical interest only, the way in which something is said being more important than what is actually meant. Not being a psychiatrist I have always been interested in the message rather than the diagnosis and Bert's messages are usually very important indeed. For example, this is what he has to say on the subject of illness and God:

> You just love the person who makes you better. Nurses, doctors. It's like God. If God lets you get poorly and you love him he makes you better. God makes you better.

This seems straightforward enough, although one does not often hear it said quite like that. What is strange, however, is Bert's attitude to the immediate reality of God. He makes it sound as if God were present in just the same way as anybody else, not as a theological assumption but as a plain ordinary fact. Bert cannot see God, but then he doesn't need to, because 'It's all God, everything's God, you know.' He certainly does not confuse himself, as an individual, with God, as people suffering from schizophrenia are sometimes supposed to do. God is Bert's fellow traveler, around the hospital and through life. The lack of structure in Bert's thinking gives his awareness of God an awe-inspiring flexibility and comprehensiveness; technically of course he is more of a poet than a theologian, but the same could be said of Henry Vaughan, Thomas Traherne, or even St John of the Cross. Bert has none of their expressive skill. What he says is notable for its meaning rather than its form. Bert's language is blunt, ramming home the splendid obviousness of God. Most people on first meeting him find him rather ridiculous and want to know why he is so happy. Poor thing, to be happy in a place like this! Surely it proves he must be ill! It's not normal to be grinning all the time!

Bert is not always grinning, however. He certainly tends to grin a lot when he is talking to people, but this is because people give him great joy. But when he is walking through the hospital grounds alone he looks quite solemn, not sad, just calmly reflective. I used to wonder what he was thinking about, something profoundly unsubtle and totally memorable—the kind of corny vision of total glory that we have categorized out of existence.

Bert'e eyes are fixed on the distant hills and the landscape through which he passes reflects their glory. Elsie sits in the garden and looks back to the past. The past is very real to Elsie, very real and very necessary, for it gives her spiritual strength to bear the burdens of the present and deal with her fears about the future. Many people in the hospital look back with longing to the days before they were admitted. It seems to them that they used to live in a totally different world from the one they now inhabit. A patient on an acute admission ward lies in bed at night, hands over ears to keep out the hospital sounds, and imagines it is his or her own bed at home. Near the hospital greenhouses an elderly gentleman stubs out a cigarette and aches to have a trowel in his hands again, his own trowel, in his own earth. Many of the patients of Elsie's generation—she is seventy-five—have completely lost touch with their families, some because their relatives have died or can no longer be traced, others because the people in question simply wanted it to be so. They intended the split to be permanent and did not want to be involved any longer with the sick person. They had been careful to do it properly. The hospital was the best place; after all, it was what it was for. For the good of all concerned he or she had been finally 'put away.' We may imagine that in a case like this a patient's thoughts of home might be characterized by a degree of resentment. As month gives way to month, year to year, decade to decade, the image of home is likely to be distorted. There is no living link between past and present, only a vague and shifting impression of love and security which somehow went horribly wrong, leaving its legacy of ingrained resentment and a terrible sense of having been betrayed.

Elsie has been spared such feelings, thank God. Her time in hospital has been unshadowed by any kind of emotional turmoil apart from the usual annoyances and small jealousies of institutional life. Her history is reflected on her face, which is smooth and unwrinkled, a characteristic of people who have lived in sheltered circumstances and avoided the wear and tear of our sink-or-swim society. In fact, she has always lived in institutions, having been brought up in an orphanage run by Dr Barnardo's. In a way this is the most important thing about Elsie, or, at least, it is what she herself considers to be most important. Even sixty years after she moved into her first job, which was some time in the 1920s, her life is built around the orphanage which was her first home. She sits on the tiny lawn in front of the immense ward-block reading her monthly letter from Barnardo's. If you show any interest at all she will tell you exactly what it says. You get the impression that Elsie still believes she is there, at the orphanage, along with all her friends. Two hundred miles and sixty years from the place she loves most, the place that is home, Elsie remains a Barnardo's girl.

Her first 'position' was as a housemaid to a doctor's family in the East End. She was very happy there for ten years; then, when she was twenty-six she left in order to get married. She does not say much about this time in her life. It appears that her husband left her soon after the birth of her first (and only) child. He was a hairdresser's

101

assistant and seems to have left Elsie for a more glamorous consort. At this critical point in her life, with a small child to look after, Barnardo's rose to the occasion and took Elsie in as a kind of junior house mother. This was another period of happiness; like the first it came to an end, although Elsie and Charlie—named after his father—did manage to stay on for several years. They would probably have stayed longer if tragedy had not struck. Playing on a rubbish dump Charlie cut his knee. The wound turned septic and within a fortnight he was dead. Nowadays, as Elsie points out, he could easily have been saved with penicillin.

Elsie left Barnardo's a second time. This time she headed north in the hope of contacting her husband's family. As it turned out it was a vain hope; she couldn't find them and, even if she had done, there was not much chance of their helping her. Her husband had severed all connection with them on first leaving home for London. Elsie did not even know if they knew he had got married. With the little boy to show them there might have been some chance. After a few weeks of scavenging from dustbins and sleeping in doorways she gave up hope of finding them. By this time she was in a wretched state, hungry, dirty and threadbare. Now, some months after Charlie's death, the full force of her loss attacked her and she literally did not know which way to turn.

A well-meaning clergyman had her admitted to the mental hospital. This man asked her where she had come from and, when she said Barnardo's, he immediately got into contact with the orphanage to inquire what he should do. Did they want him to put Elsie on a train and send her back to London? Barnardo's did not feel that they were in any position to take Elsie back again, considering the circumstances. She had left of her own free will and might decide to do so again. She was obviously in a disturbed state of mind and needed special treatment that they were not equipped to provide. Besides, they were not at all sure that Elsie would want to go home again. Had she been asked? Elsie was asked and said that she felt too guilty to return to Barnardo's and that this place—the asylum—was no more than she deserved. She was admitted on July 4th, 1930, diagnosed as suffering from depression.

Ten weeks after her admission Elsie wrote to Dr Barnardo's describing her new home and giving short pen pictures of her fellow patients and members of the hospital staff. (She didn't think she would be here for long, she said; the people were nice though not so nice as at Barnardo's and she was looking forward to seeing her old friends again.) It was the first of dozens, even hundreds, of such letters that she wrote during the next fifty-five years, at the rate of one per fortnight, with an extra one for Christmas and Easter. The wonderful thing is that her letters were always answered. There was always someone at Barnardo's to write back. Her gift for describing people and events made her letters very amusing, and this may be one of the reasons why she always received a reply. The replies were personal, addressed to Miss Elsie Brocklebank, Grange Ward, Western Meads Hospital and written in longhand rather than on a typewriter or in the form of a circular (I remember that, on one occasion, she did get a printed letter, one of the fund-raising circulars that charities send out in their thousands. Elsie was astonished to read 'Dear Miss Brocklebank' instead of 'Dear Elsie.' They never called her that! Who could have written it? She didn't recognize the name at all. They seemed to want her to send them money. I did my best to reassure her, saying it was a mistake, and not really meant for her at all. I don't think she was convinced. It was addressed to Elsie Brocklebank and there was no-one else at Western Meads called that, was there?)

I have been writing about her in the past tense, but she is still very much here with us and in her usual good health. The hospital has kept hold of her for so long because she has never tried to leave. When efforts have been made to move her into a hostel or a 'group home,' she has developed marked symptoms of depression. This is her destination, the goal of her wanderings. Sitting in the sun, thinking of Barnardo's, she contemplates the limitations of hospital life with equanimity, her spiritual home being elsewhere. In a way she represents much of the happier side of life at Western Meads. It's a hard thing to describe, this sense of grace. I think the best way of putting it would be in terms of a kind of inner harmony within the hospital as a whole. Certainly it is very much a complementary kind of experience, reconciling oppositions and restoring balances— freedom and security, submission and independence, divergence and convergence, conserving and inventing—each participating in its opposite, so that a shift of psycho-social emphasis is able to produce a new equilibrium around another point of balance.

Grahame is a charge nurse at this hospital. He has worked here for a long time; I'm not sure how long, but I think he trained at the nursing school years ago, before the Mental Health Act of 1959, when so many restrictions on the liberty of patients were lifted. Grahame is so closely identified with the hospital staff in my mind that I find it difficult to think of the one without the other. He is a large man, not fat, but heavily muscled; he 'works out' at a local health club each week and is very keen that patients should have the opportunity to take plenty of exercise. In my mind's eye I can see him leaning earnestly forward, his hands planted firmly on the desk in the office trying to persuade an elderly patient that a walk round the cricket field will do him good. Grahame and cricket are closely connected. He has been here since the time when new members of staff were expected to bring some kind of extra skill, preferably sporting or musical, to the job as well as aptitude for nursing. I think it was Grahame who established the cricket team in a series of hot summers at the end of the Second World War. Some of the team have been playing on the field alongside the chapel each summer for over thirty years, and improving all the time. Elderly men, they become suddenly young again when Grahame shoves a bat in their hands and points them towards the pitch. It seems that, when it comes to cricket, there's no substitute for knowing your pitch.

Grahame certainly knows his. Part of the skill of 'being in charge' is the ability to be totally involved in the relationship, to the extent of knowing both how to direct and be directed so that you can pass this second skill—and it is the major one—to other people. Aloofness does not help at this level, because it is only interpreted as lack of concern. I'm not sure that Grahame would really like to hear it said but he is a good charge nurse because of his protective attitude towards his patients—a very unfashionable quality in nursing. Most of the time, however, Grahame's protectiveness liberates rather than confines, because it is founded upon an authentic concern for the patients as people, who can only be understood, and consequently helped, by trying hard to identify with their feelings. People who work with those suffering from emotional illness usually share Grahame's ideals, but not everyone manages to do the job as well as he does. Some are drawn so deeply into the pain and terror that calls out to them that they are temporarily overwhelmed and retreat from the encounter in confusion, blaming themselves for their foolhardiness in allowing themselves to become involved. Others stand well clear and pride themselves on their 'professional' attitude. Their job is to carry out the doctor's instructions in a way that is kind but impersonal, refusing to allow patients to regard them as people first, staff members second. This can be just as counter-productive as the first approach, because you always need to get reasonably close to understanding how someone else feels in order to find out what is really going on in situations which involve people. No nurse likes to lose the initiative within the therapeutic relationship; but it is sometimes necessary to act in a passive, receptive way in order to sustain a relationship and, without relationship, there is no psychological healing of any kind.

Grahame manages to combine the strengths of both approaches without their weaknesses. I do not think he is conscious of his ability to be directive and supportive, detached and involved, tough and tender at the same time. I think he simply thinks he is doing his job as well as he can and that, like the rest of us, he could be doing it better. I have heard him say that he thinks the patients deserve better care than they receive from him. It's true that patients often complain about him, not through lack of care on his part, but because he has taken them to task over some matter in which they have failed to honor a promise they have made another patient, or himself. Promises are important to Grahame, because he would rather work by agreements than assigning duties. He treats each individual as a valued and respected member of the ward family to be cheered up and told off, nagged and congratulated. I particularly remember an occasion when one of his young men was unwilling to make the extra effort involved in getting up early enough to start work. It was important that he should make the effort because the job was outside the hospital, in the town and constituted a major step in Tony's rehabilitation. 'Don't think I care,' said Grahame, 'if you can't get yourself out of bed half-an-hour earlier, that's your business. It's nothing at all to do with me! It's *your* life, I'm not bothered'—but he was, and Tony knew he was. You could hear the affection in his voice belying the callousness of the words.

People sometimes resent Grahame for his personal approach. They are not used to being taken so seriously by members of staff. They are accustomed to kindness, but not to the quality of acceptance that sees them as patients second, fellow human beings first. No one carries out the business of running a ward more efficiently than he does and yet the patients feel more important, more valuable on his ward than anywhere else in the hospital. I have had patients come to me complaining of his strictness; I have never known anyone who said he was unfair. He was certainly the closest thing to a father that Tony ever had. And to a mother, too.

Grahame's own mother has always been very close to him. It was she who taught him the possibility of being father and mother at the same time, because her husband died many years ago, leaving her alone to bring Grahame up. A remarkable woman in many ways, she gave him the emotional support necessary for carrying out such a demanding job. Grahame is very much aware of how much he owes his mother and during the last few years he has had the opportunity to do something in return—something, many things—now she is getting old and rapidly becoming more and more hard to look after. A few months ago he came along with serious news. The old lady was going into a nursing home. Grahame was almost in tears. It was the last thing he wanted to happen, he said. But he knew the kind of skilled nursing care his mother needed and he could no longer give it to her himself. His job here at the hospital made it impossible. His mother had informed him that she would prefer him to spend more of his money and less of himself. He felt he had no option.

I tried to reassure him. If that was what she wanted, then it seemed to me to be the best thing. It was a decision they had arrived at together, as they usually approached difficulties and crises in their lives. Grahame said that he really believed it was what his mother wanted; he had known her long enough to be able to tell when she had made up her mind. He could not say if he wanted it too; on the one hand looking after her was so much part of his life, so that he 'wouldn't know where to put himself' without her physical presence in the house; on the other was the pressing problem of the passing of time. He was still many years off retirement.

> Sometimes I feel like giving up work and just looking after her; then I feel I can only cope *because* I've got the hospital.

I pointed out that it wasn't only his decision. They had both arrived at the same conclusion independently, although each surely knew which way the other's mind was going. Grahame described the conversation, each of them tender and decisive by turns, arriving at a conclusion which bound them closer together while outwardly determining their separation. The new arrangement has worked very well it seems. Grahame spends more time at the nursing home than at home. As he says, it is a good job he has the hospital.

This kind of balance of masculine and feminine roles is present in every female-male relationship. It is certainly the mark of a good marriage. In Grahame's case, it was the combination of roles within a single personality which drew my attention. This, too, is quite a common thing, although it is less striking in most people than it is here. To a large degree Grahame has succeeded in integrating the female unconscious element in his psyche with his conscious masculinity—obviously a valuable achievement for a nurse, whose job demands the ability to direct and to cure in almost equal parts. Many nurses—indeed all really good ones—provide evidence of this combination. Most are women but this may be because it is still a predominantly female profession; a man who chooses to be a nurse will be aware of the need to use parts of his personality which he would ignore or even despise if he were a bank clerk or a stevedore. Psychologically speaking this is a very good thing to do, just as it is good for female nurses to be made aware of their male potential. In this way we achieve a better kind of psychic balance. Society requires us to limit ourselves to the role suggested by our biological sexuality. Indeed it can be quite ruthless in doing this. But the person who has managed to integrate elements of their hidden, cross-sexual self into their conscious awareness, their ordinary everyday self will find that their relationship with life has been deepened and widened by new kinds of awareness and sensitivity.

Balance is very important. I am talking about a process of psychic cross-fertilization, not a simple take over of aspects of behavior commonly associated with the opposite sex. It is not that, by getting into contact with the other sex within themselves, men become (for example) more supportive and intuitive, women more logical and directive, although this may sometimes be the case. What happens is more to do with the achievement of greater balance and stability as elements within the psyche, which have been repressed as inappropriate for the sex concerned, are integrated with the contents of the conscious awareness. In this matter each of us achieves his or her own synthesis, as we find our own unique individual way of coming to terms with life.

As I said, nurses are noted for this kind of balanced sexual role identity. Often it is something that they bring to the job; more often, however, it is the job's gift to them. So wide are the emotional demands made upon a nurse that they find themselves developing an ability to make use of every psychic faculty at their disposal and to give public expression to aspects of themselves which our culture regards as 'un-womanly' or 'un-manly.' It is expected of them because the job demands it. Nurses have to be 'both father and mother' to their patients. I do not believe this is asking too much of them for, once we have been given permission, most of us are able to behave, and experience, in ways which reveal a richer and more flexible capability for relating to others than we ever imagined we possessed. But we need balance in order to do this. Balance and responsiveness belong together. Extreme attitudes are, by definition, self limiting, only calling forth a response from the same kind of person. A balanced approach can be the result of self-awareness, as I believe it was with Grahame.

The idea of responsiveness is fundamental to the way we understand our relationship to God.

> As the bridegroom to his chosen, as the king unto his realm,
> As the keep unto the castle, as the pilot to the helm,
> So Lord art thou to me.

These are the words of a hymn that we sing in the hospital church sometimes. They have a good deal to say about the relationship between God and his universe, and consequently about responsiveness. Response which is not free is not genuine responsiveness. In the real world, the world created in and re-created through Christ, people and things come together in harmony because they want to do so. It is world of serendipity, of falling-into-place-ness. We need not strive so hard to 'get it together,' it *is* together. Just as the human spirit yearns for the completeness of heaven, so God's enveloping love knows no remainder. Heaven and earth are made for each other. To believe this is not to deny the presence of evil, but only to assert the victory of love which makes all evil, even the most hideous, redeemable. Within the sphere of love authentic life is that which is freely exchanged. We cannot force God's hand, and he never forces ours. To do either would be to offend against the very nature of love as revealed in the life, death and rising again of Jesus.

Just as some objects are too close to the eye to be recognized, so some truths are so basic to our understanding that we find difficulty in distinguishing them as an identifiable factor in awareness. Something always happens when we try to 'take the scientific view' of life; we always move further away from life instead of closer to it. We do this because we want to be objective, to look at things as they are in themselves rather than in their relationship to us. Yet it is we who are doing the looking. The fact is that, apart from their relationship to us, things have no reality for us, which means that humanly speaking, they have no reality at all. To think and feel about a thing or a person is to make it or them a part of our own reality. Unless you are thinking and feeling, the question does not arise; when it does it is because you have humanized whatever is over against you with the gift of your awareness.

This is not the whole story, however. To leave it like this might suggest that nothing really exists apart from men and women engaged in having thoughts and feelings which bring the world into existence. Of course things and all living organisms exist as and in themselves. What I am saying is that these things have no significance for us unless we make a mental gesture towards them, and that reality is a word, an idea, which has no human meaning apart from the meaning it has for us. This always needs stating because it is almost always overlooked, being too obvious to be taken into consideration. In fact it is only a half-truth, if it is even that. This human reality, the world for us, depends upon a prior reality, an overarching meaning according to which we are bound together in relationship with whatever is not ourselves at a level which precedes our understanding about its reality.

To put this in another way, the world for us—the reality we bestow—is a world which allows us to do so. It is a world ready for understanding, one which reaches out for communication. This is not simply a poetic way of expressing the sense of belonging we have with regard to our natural environment where things 'feel right to us' because we are used to them and the world is 'ours' by virtue of our being born into it. The French psychologist Marcel Merleau-Ponty claims that there is an actual concordance between ourselves and nature in terms of the relationship of subject and object: 'The sensations and images that should be the beginning and end of all knowledge'—the ways we perceive the world, that is—'never make their appearances anywhere other than within a horizon of meaning' (Merleau-Ponty, 1962). We do not make sense of things by ourselves; sense is waiting for us within the things we perceive when we look about us, when we feel the grass beneath our feet and touch the sawn plank on the carpenter's bench. From these things, meaning reaches out to us and takes us to itself. Thus the truth of ordinary human perception is neither within us nor within the natural world of other people and things; it is among and around us ordering our thoughts in its own image, and what goes on is more of a collaboration than something invented by us or imposed on us.

This, I suppose, is how I see the hospital. I have ideas about it which I have learned from the things I have read and been told. I make assumptions about it based on what 'everybody' knows and feels about asylums and mental clinics of any kind. I have feelings about it which originate in my having been a patient on a locked ward in a place like this. And yet the hospital is itself. It is more than, and different from, my ideas, assumptions, feelings. It speaks to me and I listen. I respond. The hospital is itself, a place of contrasts, an unique combination of characteristic situations, events and people—not the idea of such a thing, but the thing itself, the *actual* thing. I do not have to surrender my critical faculty when I regard it but there is no way I can encounter it without being affected by its life. The building itself, its wards and passages, its stone walls and classical cornice has life. The intention to help and heal is built into this place waiting to be recognized and understood rather than simply dismissed or used in the service of private fantasy. A whole history of helping and caring lies behind each cup of ward tea, every arm round somebody's shoulder, every injection. For criticism to be a genuine expression of humanness it must be founded in experience of the thing itself. It should never be a culturally-induced record from a taboo-object.

I can be as critical as I like about Western Meads and places like it. I can be aware of what seems, by our current Western standards of evaluation, the large scale waste of human potential involved in keeping people incarcerated who are no longer mentally ill, or are only intermittently so. I can agree with those who point out that shutting up those who are ill along with other people in the same condition may have the effect of making them worse. I can also deplore the attitudes and policies of a society that deals with people whom it claims to care about—patients, ill people—by making sure it will never come into contact with them. I, too, can remember what it is like to be shut up and left and not know when I will get out, if ever.

But I have met the hospital on its own terms, and I can never feel quite the same again. For one thing, I'm no longer sure that giving mentally ill people the security and safety, the feeling of being on an island away from the world is a bad thing. It may result in a degree of psychological regression—but what if they need the opportunity to grow up again in safety? The idea of 'wasted lives' may apply to some patients, but as a kind of blanket description it is nonsense. Who, after all, judges whether a life is wasted or not? Many of these people lived lives full of friendship and love. The amount they contributed to their community could be gauged by the size of the congregations that came to their funerals in the Hospital Church. Certainly the hospital had few visitors, but this was certainly not because it discouraged them; whether they were relatives or not, they were always made extremely welcome. Ward Sisters and Charge Nurses went out of their way to encourage people to visit the patients on their wards. If very few came, whose fault was that? Will they have more visitors when they leave?

Because they are leaving. The hospital, with all the others like it, is closing down. Western Meads is in the process of being destroyed. We are losing more than buildings.

7 EPILOGUE

It would be easy to be sentimental about what was happening, easier still to let sentimentality blind one to the ordinary reality of the situation within the hospital, when people improvise therapeutic routines to fit the reduced circumstances imposed upon them. The shortage of nurses affected everyone, even the chaplain; elderly patients are not allowed off their wards to attend the Sunday Service because the entire ward has to be taken to the toilet in strict rotation, this being the most labor-intensive method. Saying the 'short' Communion on each ward is not the best way of doing things because people, especially these people, like to be members of a congregation, but it is a way of keeping the church's life going in reduced circumstances.

The objective of the hospital as a whole is to 'ride the changes,' not to be panicked into the kind of action which would leave people faced with mental illness with nowhere to turn, no place where they could find help, either for themselves or their families when life at home became impossible—no alternative to the railway arches, in fact. We are all familiar with the usual stereotypes of mentally ill people needing help: the acutely ill teenager who needs immediate treatment away from his or her parents; the elderly man or woman, exiled from the hospital which has been his or her home for so many years, trying to cope, on the one hand, with three or four friends in a house in a suburban street where people rarely talk to one another anyway, on the other, in a seaside bed and breakfast on their own; the victim of Alzheimer's disease whose aged husband or wife simply cannot cope and has to have on-going help. Each situation affects other people apart from the person categorized as mentally ill, people who are under increasing emotional pressure and need immediate relief. At the time of writing the hospital existed in order to give such relief, to both those who are ill and those who, if the situation continues, soon may be.

Discouraged from rapid action by a lack of consensus among the local authorities, and also by its own characteristic conservatism, Western Meads took its time. There was no rapid expulsion of large numbers such as had happened in some parts of the country. During the 1980s, a special team of psychologists and rehabilitation experts had been introduced into the hospital and, at the time of writing, there were five hundred patients instead of the fifteen hundred who had been here fifteen years ago. What has happened to them? Of the men and women with controllable chronic illnesses, who are able to receive treatment at the hands of their local doctors, many live in rented accommodation or 'bed and breakfast' hotels. These are the ex-patients who cannot be looked after by their relatives, either because they no longer have a family willing and able to take responsibility for them, or—and this is frequently the case—their relatives abandoned them many years ago, when they first came into hospital.

Other ex-patients have not been so fortunate. The men and women who hang around the hospital gates or come in to meet their friends at the tea bar have had to settle for a lonely life in a council flat on the immense estate outside the hospital. They are not in a position to write to me from coastal resorts—even if the letters do sometimes ask if I can get the writer re-admitted! The presence of 'mental patients' has always been a cause of anxiety and distress to those who live in this city. After all, at the Meads we are on their doorstep. Now that the threshold has been crossed, there is no way that we can be successfully ignored. Because ex-patients do not have jobs, being considered unemployable, they spend a lot of time walking round the town or sitting in cafes and pubs. Anyone who is not engaged in some obviously identifiable occupation—who looks lonely, or bored with whatever is going on around him or her—such a person is likely to be looked at askance and regarded with the slightly fascinated disdain reserved for psychiatric patients: 'do you think he's from down the road?' Whether or not, better leave him alone, because you never know.

The men and women in question know, however. People who have spent time as patients at Western Meads are under no illusion as to how they stand, or rather lodge, in the inhospitable, rejecting neighborhoods to which they have been exiled. Some of them made use of the two 'drop-in centers' opened in the town. At least, these are the ones I meet, having extended my sphere of operations beyond the hospital gates. At the center run by the local branch of MIND, a group of ex-patients have organized themselves into an amateur self-help collective. Generally speaking there are more skills among them than resources to back them up, but there are always one or two who simply cannot help themselves and depend on the rest to keep going at all. Half of a small terraced house—the other half belongs to a society for helping alcoholics—two up and two down, rescued from the demolishers and renovated by schoolchildren, is both outpost and headquarters for a group of people each of whom has 'done time' at Western Meads. It would be too expensive to keep it open for more than three days a week but, while it is, it provides a cheap meal and an opportunity to talk to people who are willing to bother to find out what you mean.

These are just glimpses of the state of affairs that existed. I do not claim to be unbiased and objective. It's hard to be those things with your world crumbling beneath you. Writing this in the closing years of the 1980s, as my professional career drew towards its end, I found myself in the midst of a desperate state of affairs, desperate for me because it represented the total defeat of everything I had worked for and believed in during my time as a chaplain, even more so for the patients and families involved. I was left with a series of unanswered questions. *Do* long-stay patients want to be discharged from hospital? Some do, I know, because I've spoken to them; I've spoken to many more who do not, who are terrified of the future away from the place and the people they know. I've spoken to desperate people, bewildered people, people who felt betrayed. Most of the patients however were simply stunned. Nothing remotely like this had happened to them before in their protected, predictable lives in the hospital. I suspect that these are the ones who try to commit suicide—often, I'm afraid, succeeding. Are there families and neighborhoods that welcome them? I'm sure there must be! It's just that I don't see it happening, and there is no reason why I should. Many ex-patients must simply start on a new happily domestic chapter, glad to be restored to the family circle. On the other hand what about the relatives who never visited, and now have to make arrangements involving considerably more than that? Lionel, who had been in hospital since his teens and was now well over sixty said to me one morning, 'do you think they're able to sleep in their beds at night? Because of God and Jesus?' He had not been talking about the family who put him into hospital all those years ago, but that is what he meant. What about the bitterness and the guilt? The culture-shock? The sheer inability to cope with the demands of life outside? Is it possible, is it credible, that a new way of living with mental breakdown could emerge from so much pain and callous disregard for the humanity of others less fortunate than ourselves? Certainly, this is what the authorities were encouraging us to hope for! But was this genuine, or a cover-up? Is it, after all, simply another horrifying failure of love, which is how I myself now see it?

To be fair, very little clear thinking seems to have gone into finding an answer to the problem of mental illness. This is a subject that people find it hard to be rational about. It is a kind of limiting condition of human understanding—a concept so complete that it gets in the way of the living human beings it is supposed to refer to. We know less about someone when we know that he or she is mentally ill than we did before, because we can no longer trust what

117

we thought we knew. Perhaps, too, we have been institutionalized by the hospitals which have made madness so exotic that we have no idea how to deal with it. Shut away behind high walls, banished to the outskirts of cities, handed over to highly trained specialists, the mentally ill possess their own kind of glamor; once they lose the fascination of the unknown and the forbidden, they take us unawares, and we panic. It was not only convenient to build these hospitals out in the countryside, it was also highly significant. The distance which protected us physically involved us emotionally, in that it exerted a powerful imaginative force upon us, exaggerating the terrifying otherness of the mentally ill, and the hospital symbolizing their pitiable condition. I can remember my own parents threatening to 'send for the cab, to have you taken to Hillside.' Hillside was twenty miles away; in my imagination, however, it was just around the corner. I wasn't the only child chastened in this way; there were Hillsides all over the country fulfilling the same disciplinary role in a million households.

It is people like this, people who have this attitude to mental illness, who are now supposed to take over the care of the emotionally disturbed. Instead of asylums, we have the occasional drop-in center. Instead of nurses we have men and women painstakingly educated into an irrational attitude towards madness, an attitude to which they cling because it has the safety of long familiarity, and also because it carries with it a reflexive reassurance about their own rationality. For, as I have already said, in a culture which sets so much store on intelligence, people are determined to retain the concept of the mental patient, as a kind of base-line human condition, a social nadir, the one human status that can't be undercut or downstaged.

As we have seen, people have a deeply rooted terror of mental illness and cling to the precious image of themselves as rational individuals, totally in charge of all their precious faculties. It is a precarious position, and one which we may never be entirely certain that we can keep our hold on, but heaven forbid that we should ever completely lose our grip. Fear of madness is fear of the abyss, the unknown experienced as the unknowable. It can only be compared with our attitude towards our own death. Death, however, can be seen as an end which gives shape to our life, creating meaning from the flux of events; madness is by definition a denial of sense, and renders all previous life, all valuable personal events, futile. It is not just a unreasonable happening, but something which puts the meaning of reason itself in question. Madness is personal disaster.

This is why psychiatric hospitals have such power over our imagination. The madhouse is a more fitting symbol of our deepest and least eradicable loathings than the graveyard, the torture chamber or the prison. It contains elements of all these separate hells of the imagination, combined with its own distinctive anti-rational horror. Neither Hillside nor Western Meads was actually like this, of course, but, as I have already said, we are dealing with fantasy, not fact, here. However many doors are unlocked, however many wards opened, Western Meads remains outside the real world. Even as it is shut down, it is in process of being re-invented.

The myth of madness abides, sending a shiver down people's backs when the conductor calls out 'Asylum Corner,' dissuading relatives from visiting patients and employers from giving ex-patients jobs, and bestowing a strange unwelcome glamor on those of us who work here. It persists everywhere in the world of mental illness, in specially established 'therapeutic communities' or the brand-new psychiatric wings of District General Hospitals. In great suburban asylums like Hillside and Western Meads it lingers as an ineradicable atmosphere, a wind from the past blowing round gray stone buttresses and whispering along half deserted corridors and in day rooms newly decorated with bright wallpaper and cheerful prints. No amount of upgrading, either physical or spiritual, seems able to disperse it.

Most of all, it persists in the day-to-day relationships of ex-patients with the people they now meet in the course of their ordinary lives, the people of the town. It is this that enables it to infect the hostels and drop-in centers where ex-patients gather together, however domestic and un-institutional such places set out to be. Proximity to ex-patients is seen as socially degrading, so that even those who feel compassion towards the mentally ill prefer to keep their distance from them, because of the ancient stigma attached to their condition; people like that *ought* to be kept on their own. Wherever a hostel is built, property prices fall. Evidence of their 'cure,' presented by their ability to keep ordinary social rules and live ordinary domestic lives, turns out to be even more threatening because it shows an insidious ability to take on the appearance of normality, a threatening tendency to be less alien—if they are more like us, perhaps we are more like them!

People who are in the grip of a powerful myth, anthropologists say, are divided from their fellow men and women by exactly such pressures as these. Whichever way they turn, they are separated from ordinary society. During my last months I came to see my role as a psychiatric chaplain as a kind of cultural exorcist, working in two directions at once. On the one hand I worked towards lifting the curse of ex-patienthood from the men and women who have left hospital and are trying to come to terms with life 'outside.' I must admit that I have not done half as much in this direction as some other priests particularly those who have managed to extend their sphere of action to become 'community psychiatric chaplains,' working hard to establish more places where ex-patients can find congenial company and professional support. The Christian church is ideally organized for this kind of enterprise, and I have heard of several centers and clubs which have been established in neighborhoods close to psychiatric hospitals, often on an ecumenical basis. We did not get so far as this. Although some local clergy showed interest, most expressed good will and left it at that, so that I worked mainly in the day centers set up by MIND and the social services, in co-operation with the health authority. The purpose of these centers was not to act as psychiatric clinics but as meeting places for conversation and mutual encouragement, with a view to establishing a sense of personal autonomy and individual worth.

Psychological help is available, of the kind that many people can benefit from, whether ex-patients or not.

On the other hand, I tried to reach as many people as I could, both individually and in groups, in order to persuade them to re-think established attitudes about mental illness, mental hospitals and former mental patients. I talked to a range of audiences, mainly church groups but also secular bodies—schools, discussion groups, prisoners and prison officers, Rotarians, etc.—and was almost always received with understanding and sometimes with enthusiasm. I think that my own personal history has added weight to my words, but I also feel that much of the impact has been due to the message of deliverance which I have been entrusted with as a minister of the Gospel. This was the message I tried to put across to a wider audience in 'Patients and People,' a television program about my work at Western Meads which was presented in January 1987.

The Chaplain is engaged in a struggle against ideas which have a demonic power over men's lives. He does not have to fight alone, however. It may sometimes seem to him that the presence which establishes the dominant interpretation of the meaning of mental illness—the mythology of madness—is all-powerful and must prevail over any efforts he or anybody else can make to fight against it. But the system is made up of people and it is people who triumph, Again and again, during my life at Western Meads, I was brought face to face with a fact which alters every theoretical assumption which I, and others like me, may have about mental illness. The simple fact of kindness.

I came to Western Meads with vivid memories of another hospital, partly expecting to find here an atmosphere of repression and fear. I hoped that I would be proved wrong. Indeed it was to 'lay that ghost' that I took the job. That ghost has been well and truly laid. From the day I arrived I was aware of a curious warmth, an unexpected sense of comradeship, pervading the whole hospital.

Simple camaraderie, the awareness of being 'all together against the world' certainly isn't the whole explanation, although it is probably part of it. There was a quality of warmth and of kindness here which is more than a sociological phenomenon, a corporate ego defense on the part of a psychologically threatened sub-group. Love was shown in many ways throughout the hospital, given and received in wards and workshops, occupational therapy departments and treatment. This love is not confined to hospitals. It is this love that will prevail.

BIBLIOGRAPHY

Bourne, H. (1958, 1 May). Insulin coma in decline. *American Journal of Psychiatry 114*, 1015-1017.

Faber, H. (1971). *Pastoral care in the modern hospital*. London: SCM Press. Translation by Hugo de Waal of *De pastor in het moderne ziekenhuis*.

Grainger, R. (1979). *Watching for wings: theology and mental illness in a pastoral setting*. London: Darton, Longman and Todd.

Grainger, R. (2009). *Laying the ghost: patients into users*. London: Chipmunka.

Merleau-Ponty, M. (1962). *Phenomenology of perception*. London/ New York: Routledge & Kegan Paul/Humanities Press. Translation by Colin Smith of *Phénoménologie de la perception*.

Winfield, S. (1983). *Open Mind*. National Association for Mental Health, 5.